Off and Walking

Off and Walking

A hiker's guide to American places

by Ruth Rudner

HOLT, RINEHART AND WINSTON
New York

Published simultaneously in Canada by Holt, Rinehart
and Winston of Canada, Limited.

Library of Congress Cataloging in Publication Data

Rudner, Ruth.
    Off and walking.

    Bibliography: p.
    1. Backpacking.   2. Backpacking—United States.
I. Title.
GV199.6.R8   796.5   76–29913
ISBN 0–03–015596–7
ISBN 0–03–015591–6 pbk.

FIRST EDITION

Designer: Betty Binns
Maps by Deborah Peretz
Photographs by Ruth Rudner

PRINTED IN THE UNITED STATES OF AMERICA
10   9   8   7   6   5   4   3   2   1

Acknowledgments

My thanks to the people who helped me gather background information and who then, later, took time out of the beginning of what was expected to be—because of the Bicentennial—the busiest summer ever in the National Parks and Forests to go over the information included in the tours. Mary M. Reynolds of Olympic National Park; James Sleznick, Jr., of Yosemite National Park; R. M. "Jim" Nelson of the U.S. Forest Service, Lakewood, Colorado, who checked the chapter on Uncompahgre National Forest; Carol Koepcke who is now at Crater Lake National Park, but who was my resource in the Tetons while she was there; John M. Morehead of Isle Royale National Park; Ned Therrien of the White Mountain National Forest; and Donald H. DeFoe of Great Smoky Mountains National Park were all enormously helpful with their suggestions, comments, and updated facts. Patrick Finney of the U.S. Forest Service in Lakewood also provided useful and plentiful information.

And my thanks to all those people, whose names I will never know, who give rides to hitchhiking hikers en route to or from a hike. You have saved me endless miles of concrete in the friendliest of ways.

To the people whose names I know well, who hike with me, my thanks for the things you have taught me. I have been glad of your company.

A few photos in the book were snapped by hiking companions and occasional passing strangers. The photo on p. 1 is by Jim Goldsmith.

To Brian, Jason, Kayla, Michael, and Lisa
who inherit our paths

with my love,
Ruth

The aim of a book may be to instruct,
Yet you can also use it as a pillow. . . .

—JALALUDIN RUMI

Contents

Preface

Before the summer of 1975 when I made most of the hikes described in this book, my summers were spent hiking from hut to hut in the Alps. Backpacking was confined to other seasons and the east of America. West of West Virginia lay an unknown land that I envisaged as a maze of superhighways bypassing fading towns whose names nobody could remember. An occasional desert or range of wild mountains seemed unutterably far away. America was too vast. I valued the intimacy of Europe with its mountains and towns, its remote valleys and historic cities closely connected by footpaths, trains, buses, and centuries of tradition.

America *is* vast. But if the whole of it is too large for intimacy, the parts of it are a different matter. In each group of mountains and the towns around it I found the ambience I sought: wildness and civilization, open to me, ready for me to experience in their American forms, set in relief by great distances of empty road between.

This book, the outcome of that journey of discovery, is meant for those who like mountain hiking for the challenge and adventure and whatever solitude is available, and afterward the amenities of pleasant towns, civilized places that provide the sense of being on a journey rather than of merely passing through.

Some of the actual routes described are ideal for novice back-packers, others are for more experienced hikers or backpackers, but all are intended to serve as examples of what can be done by anyone. Each of the hikes relates, somewhere along the way, to some place. That place can be a town or village or even a lodge or hotel atmospheric enough to stand in the stead of a town. The important thing is that it be a pleasant spot to come upon and lay down one's pack in. On the other hand, if you've no mind for such civilized places, all the tours can be made without ever stepping foot in any one of them.

The information in Part One should be useful in planning your trip, whether it is to one of the regions described or to an-other area entirely. The tour descriptions in Part Two, taken from the diaries I kept on each one, can be used as guides for anyone making the same trip, or as background information for anyone wanting to map out his own trip in the same area. Where they exist, I have also listed guidebooks for these regions. Part Three is an expression of my own concern about the overuse and preser-vation of our extraordinary backcountry. If you are not an ex-perienced backpacker, there are a number of thorough, technical books on the subject that will be useful to you. A list of them ap-pears in Appendix A. In the appendixes you will also find miscel-laneous information about other books, lodging, pack stock, some useful addresses, etc.

Between the time of writing this book and its publication some facts along the various ways may have changed. They were chang-ing even during the writing. Nevertheless, the basic structure of the tours described remains the same. So does the experience of a journey by foot. The grandeur and the delicacy, the eternal newness of the natural world; the rage and softness of its weather and seasons; the ease, the occasional discomfort, the simplicity of living within it—eternally changing, these things remain the same.

PART ONE

THE GROUNDWORK

1 Mountains and civilization

Civilization is not unnatural to man. In the Caucasus or the Himalayas, the Rockies or the Alps, it is not unnatural for man to have built farms and villages in high, remote valleys. Alone on some jagged, treeless peak, I find it agreeable to see a distant sunlit valley, its fields a patchwork of greens around neat towns. If I resent ever having to come down to the towns, I do, at least, enjoy their amenities once I'm there. I also prefer that they be pretty.

HUT SYSTEMS

Sometimes it is not necessary to come down to towns to enjoy certain civilized comforts. In Europe miles and miles of trails throughout the mountains are linked by huts in which, on even the most remote of alps, the hiker finds food and lodging. All the huts are simple, rustic structures, some ruder than others. How-

3

ever rough, the comfort the huts offer at the end of a long, hard day's hike seems only to heighten the challenge of Europe's mountains. It certainly adds to the freedom of wandering in them when, not burdened by a 40-pound pack, one can easily bend down to investigate a wild flower or some odd bug.

In the U.S. the idea of a hut system has to battle a survival tradition born of our beginnings as wilderness pioneers. Unwilling to let go of the trappings of that heritage (although the pioneers did fast enough), we often get pleasure not so much from just being in a wild world, but from playing house in it. Nature itself, and often enough hiking as well, takes second place to the process of surviving the wilderness night under (hopefully) the stars. Nevertheless, on a small scale, huts do exist. In the Appalachian Mountain Club (AMC) huts in New Hampshire's White Mountains and in the tent-hotels in Yosemite, we have two separate systems of linked huts where lodging and meals are available to travelers by foot. The AMC is the oldest hiking club in America, dating from 1876, and Yosemite is one of the oldest National Parks, established in 1890—proving, possibly, that some comfort does come with age.

There are isolated huts in other places as well, like the two in Glacier National Park, which make it possible to have that spectacular country without having to camp in it. They are, unfortunately, not linked by trails to each other. Both huts, the Granite Park Chalet at 6,700 feet near the park's center and the Sperry Chalet, south of Granite Park at 6,500 feet, were built before 1920 and are primitive, friendly refuges similar to the European huts. (Addresses are in Appendix C.) A hut system has been proposed for the still uncompleted Colorado Trail, 550 miles extending from Denver to Durango.

Along a 50-mile stretch of Vermont's Long Trail, six country inns and farms have joined together to offer bed and board to hikers who don't mind going several miles off the trail to find them. For further information, write: Country Inns along the Trail, c/o Churchill House Inn, RFD No. 3, Brandon, Vermont 05733.

TOWNS

As for old and charming towns, Colorado, New Hampshire, and Vermont have them in plenty. Here you can hike in mountains and come to, somewhere nearby, wonderful towns like Silverton, Colorado; Woodstock, Vermont; Jackson, New Hampshire—towns with histories of their own. These towns, and many others like them, have maintained, or re-created, their character so strongly that one cannot help but get a firm sense of place. I find that otherwise, often in America, out of the backcountry, I do not know where I am. Of course, that's highly subjective—I have a great longing for real places.

Many Americans take their "places" with them. In National Parks summer roads are jammed with trailers; along all the western highways the greater part of traffic is trailers, each one bigger than the one before, sometimes trailer pulling trailer. Signs on the backs of trailers announce, HI. WE'RE THE JOE DOES FROM TOPEKA, or HAVE A NICE DAY. Once, in Shenandoah, forced to tent in a campground also used by trailers, I saw one with a wrought-iron sign planted in the ground in front of it saying THE JOHN SMITHS. Commercial lodging is expensive and trailers are often the only way possible to take a vacation. But there is something insular about it, as if we could not break out of our own places, could view the world only from the security of them. We are perpetual travelers on highways that put out no welcome but merely tolerate us because we possess a vehicle. Road builders, we have engineered a society that passes through everywhere, that has no mind for intimacy.

2 How to figure out where to go if you've never been there

BOOKS AND PAMPHLETS

If hiking a route of huts interests you, then the choice is easy, since it consists of just the White Mountains or Yosemite. But if you want to make a backpacking trip, how do you find out what the possibilities are out of your own region? That is, where *is* the wilderness? Ideally, there should be a central agency in the U.S. dispensing *all* available information to hikers, but instead there are two helpful books and a number of pamphlets.

The Handbook of Wilderness Travel by George S. Wells, published by Colorado Outdoor Sports Corp., Denver, and *Wilderness Areas of North America* by Ann and Myron Sutton, published by Funk & Wagnalls, New York, both list backcountry areas. Mr. Wells describes them in every state where they exist and includes information on methods of wilderness travel (backpacking, pack trips, canoeing), information on some national scenic and recreational trails such as the Pacific Crest and Appalachian trails, and a directory of outdoor clubs. The Suttons' book describes wilderness areas by regions, including Canada, Mexico, and Central America. Both books give addresses for further information, and both are available in paperback.

The U.S. Department of Agriculture Forest Service pamphlet "Search for Solitude" (PA–942; 65¢) descriptively lists National Forests and their Wilderness Areas (although the very newest may not be included in the current issue), but gives no addresses. Regional headquarters and a list of National Forests in the states with which this book is concerned are given in Appendix B. The U.S. Department of the Interior National Park Service pamphlet "Back-Country Travel in the National Park System" (S/N 2405–0267; 80¢) lists, with addresses, National Monuments and Recreational Areas as well as National Parks.

The U.S. Forest Service and the National Park Service jointly publish the pamphlet "National Scenic and Recreational Trails" (S/N 2416–0077; 60¢), listing those trails with their location and mileage. This pamphlet includes a large number of routes besides the previously mentioned Pacific Crest and Appalachian trails. There are such wonders as the Lewis and Clark Trail from Illinois to the Pacific, the Santa Fe Trail from Missouri to Santa Fe, the North Country Trail from Vermont to North Dakota, and so on and on. The pamphlet is useful as an indication of where these long and sometimes historic trails exist, but is in no way descriptive of them. You must still inquire further for detailed information.

These pamphlets and a list of others with their prices are all available from the Superintendent of Documents, U.S. Government Printing Office, Washington, D.C. 20402. You must allow plenty of time to receive them, since several months can elapse between your request (with a check enclosed) and their arrival. Even then, you are apt to receive the wrong one.

If you know which state interests you, you may find the fastest way to get information about hiking in it is to write that state's chamber of commerce with a request for information about its National Parks and Forests. Then write directly to the park or forest headquarters for their free information (which, for National

Parks and occasional Forests, includes a small map that shows trails, shelters, major points of interest, and roads, but not topographical features). Remember to ask for a list of their guidebooks and the topographic maps that cover the areas. (In the case of California you must inquire directly of the individual parks, since the chamber of commerce no longer supports a department of tourism there.) Topographic maps exist for all National Park areas and for some National Forests. Guidebooks sometimes exist. Where they do, they are generally available only in shops of the region or in the park visitor centers. If you've planned far enough ahead, you have time to order them from the visitor center. A number of areas are covered by Sierra Club Totebooks (see list in Appendix A), which are available in bookstores and backpacking shops nationwide, or from the Sierra Club, 530 Bush Street, San Francisco, California 94108.

Once you arrive in an area, take time to visit the local backpacking shop. You will often find additional guides there to trails in the region but outside the park or forest you've chosen. You might change your whole hike.

NATIONAL TRAILS COUNCIL

While you are waiting for your information to arrive, you may have time to consider that ideal agency for hikers. The framework for it does exist. The National Trails Council, with headquarters in Chicago, *should* (and one day hopefully will) be able to function as a hiker's information service for the entire country. Currently it is a volunteer organization with no funds except those from membership fees. It can only pass on a request for information to the appropriate trail organization from whom you may or may not ever hear.

The National Trails Council was born of a 1971 meeting (National Trails Symposium) sponsored by the Departments of Agriculture and the Interior (that is, the Forest Service and the

National Park Service) along with the Open Lands Project of Chicago. With that background, why shouldn't this central information agency be able to obtain the relatively small amount of money necessary to make it into a real and useful service to hikers? Support by potential users of National Trails Council information generating enough activity in its behalf—i.e., getting across a strong enough message to Congress and to the Park and Forest services—might do it. The European countries have long supplied detailed hiking information in a centralized way via their respective national alpine clubs.

For membership and other information about the National Trails Council, write to them at: 53 West Jackson Boulevard, Chicago, Illinois 60604.

MAPS

The United States Geological Survey (part of the Interior Department) issues maps for all National Parks and a good deal of the rest of America. Indexes showing available maps for each state and territory (should you decide to hike in American Samoa or Antarctica) are obtainable free. For maps of areas east of the Mississippi, write: Branch of Distribution, U.S. Geological Survey, 1200 South Eads Street, Arlington, Virginia 22202. For maps of areas west of the Mississippi, write: Branch of Distribution, U.S. Geological Survey, Federal Center, Denver, Colorado 80225. Also free at the same addresses is information describing available topographic maps and explaining both the markings on the maps and the map symbols.

Maps come in several series (sizes/scales). Size is sometimes given in minutes: 7.5-minute series (scale, 1:24,000) in which 1 inch represents 2,000 feet or 2½ inches represents 1 mile; 15-minute series (scale, 1:62,500) in which 1 inch represents almost 1 mile. In the U.S. 1:125,000 series (scale, 1:125,000) 1 inch represents almost 2 miles; in the U.S. 1:250,000 series (scale,

1:250,000), 1 inch represents nearly 4 miles. *Scale* on a map means the relationship between the distance on the map and the corresponding distance on the ground, which means that the smaller the series number, the larger the scale (i.e., the smaller the area covered, the larger are the specific things covered). The larger the scale, the easier the map is to read, but you may need more than one map in that case to provide a complete picture of the area where you plan to hike.

A map series consists of a group of maps that conform to established specifications for size, scale, content, etc. But maps are also identified by quadrangles. A quadrangle—which, in fact, *is* a map—covers a 4-sided area bounded by parallels of latitude and meridians of longitude. The size of a quadrangle is given in minutes or degrees (i.e., the series) and defines the number of square miles covered by the map.

Some areas are covered by more than one quadrangle. This means these areas are represented by two or more maps published in different scales (that is, different series). Although scale differs, all the quadrangles for a single area will have the same name. Once you choose which quadrangle seems most useful to you and are ready to order a map, you must include the quadrangle name and series designation (7.5 minute, 15 minute, 1:250,000, etc.) and, for clarity's sake, you might also include the state.

All maps do not always show all hiking trails. Often new trails have been built since the map was published. Unless the map bears a recent publishing date, make sure you also get hold of local maps for the area where you plan to hike. Even without all the trails marked, topo maps do give you an accurate picture of the terrain, essential for cross-country hiking. In areas for which there are no topo maps, you will also have to obtain local maps, usually available at local outdoor equipment stores.

Maps may be ordered from the two addresses previously listed, depending on whether they are for areas east or west of the

Mississippi. Allow at least two weeks for delivery. Many are also available at map stores, bookstores, sporting-goods stores, etc., throughout the country. They are usually cheaper from the government. You must send a check or money order with your order. Maps in the 7.5- or 15-minute series cost 75¢; 1:250,000 cost $1.00; 1:125,000 varies: Yosemite and Olympic National Parks each cost $1.00, Great Smoky Mountains National Park costs $1.25, Isle Royale National Park costs $1.50, and Grand Teton National Park costs $2.50.

It is also possible to purchase a kit of all the topo maps of a specific area without having to put them together yourself. It costs more, but could be a convenience if you've not yet pinpointed the exact route of your hike. Wilderness Sports Corp., Eagle Valley, New York 10974, offers a free catalog of all its map kits.

SELECTING A GATEWAY

The gateway to the backcountry can be one of those civilized places mentioned earlier, a town or hotel that provides you with a beginning, or it can be the actual entrance to a park. Whatever it is, you have to get to it. If you are dependent on public transportation, you will have to select it in advance of your arrival. Based on where public transportation will take you, you may even have to choose your route or the general area of your route before you get to the region. A car makes you more flexible, allowing you to travel around the region a little before deciding on a place to start, although you still might want to have some idea what town or lodge or campground to aim for. Where backcountry permits are required, you must be near enough a ranger station to obtain the permit before beginning your hike.

It would be easiest to select a route, and thus a gateway, if you could sit down with guidebook and topo map in hand. But there may be no guidebook for a particular area. Then, too, until you know where you are going, or have narrowed it down to a few choices, it may be difficult to know which topo map or maps to purchase.

To make the broader choice of an area, you might arbitrarily pick one region rather than another simply because you are in the mood for a certain landscape—rain forest or desert, for instance. If the area is within a National Park or Forest, you can write for their maps. You might then, just as arbitrarily, select a route from the park's or forest's map because it goes from one place to another, or because it can be done as a circular route, or because it includes the highest point in the region or avoids it, etc.

From the park's or forest's information you can gather the name of a town to head for. Lists of accommodations in that town and the surrounding region are available from the town's chamber of commerce or from the state's chamber of commerce. It would be prudent to book lodging there ahead of time, or at least to phone ahead early in the day. If in summer you have not booked in advance and arrive late, you will invariably be told at the first few motels that at this hour, in this season, it will be difficult to find anything. It is perhaps even more difficult to find space in campgrounds, most of which in resort areas are reserved months in advance. (By campgrounds I mean, specifically, drive-in areas with trailer hookups and facilities for tenting, for which a fee is charged. Some guides to campgrounds are listed in Appendix C.) Keep at it. Ask the motel clerks for suggestions. There is, almost always, *something* off in some odd corner of town.

3   Working out a route

In areas where there is one, head for the ranger station or visitor center. If you have already mapped out a route, go over it with the ranger, who may or may not make some suggestions, and pick up your backcountry permit if one is required.

BACKCOUNTRY PERMITS

While permits are not required everywhere, they have come to be expected in most protected backcountry areas. They can be obtained free from either the National Park Service or the U.S. Forest Service in the area you plan to hike. They are sometimes available by mail, sometimes only in person. (Write or phone the park or forest before your trip to get current regulations.) Backcountry permits usually require that you select an itinerary and stick to a specific schedule, although within that schedule you may have a choice of routes. For more flexibility you might plan a layover day or two along your route. If you have not worked out an itinerary, the ranger will help you, but you should have either an idea of where you want to go or a willingness to put yourself wholly in his or her hands.

Your permit will usually specify a certain campsite or zone for each night of your hike. Campsites (called "backcountry campsites" or "camping areas" or "zones" in wilderness management jargon) are areas that can be reached only by unmechanized means—foot, horse, canoe, etc. They may have a shelter, outhouse, and/or fire circles, but they are otherwise undeveloped. Some National Parks and Wilderness Areas of National Forests allow a certain percentage of these campsites to be reserved in advance, often as early as January or February for a summer trip. The remaining percentage is held for first come, first served. While this generally works out so that even if there is no more space in the campsite you request—i.e., the one logical for the route you've chosen—there *is* space in a reasonable alternative. The ranger can work it out for you.

Permits serve two main purposes. One is the promotion of your safety. Since they must be obtained from the people responsible for the backcountry (rangers or seasonal employees working with the rangers), you will be able to get accurate information about trail conditions. If you've chosen an impassable route, the ranger will suggest an alternate route or tell you if you need special equipment. If you should be injured or lost from your party, a properly filled-out permit (that has been adhered to) will provide the information necessary to begin a search-and-rescue effort.

A second purpose of your permit is to provide statistics about backcountry use (low use as well as overuse) and a way of imposing use limits on overused areas. If you choose an overused area, the ranger will suggest an alternate route. If you choose an area whose permit quota for campsite space is full, you will *have* to choose an alternate route. But in small parks, like Grand Teton National Park, unless you've reserved campsite space in advance, you could find yourself with *no* possible alternatives and, therefore, no overnight hiking route at all.

ADVANCE RESERVATIONS

Advance reservations for shelter space are also common along major hiking routes like the Appalachian Trail. Since camping is often not allowed in the vicinity of these shelters, any route incorporating the trail requires some advance planning. Advance reservations are essential for all huts and the tent-hotels in Yosemite National Park.

When you write or phone any park or forest for information, inquire about advance reservations for campsites. If they are suggested, you will have to work out the route as best you can from the park's or forest's information long before you arrive at your gateway, then contact the ranger's office once again and ask them to make suggestions about campsites for you to reserve.

STICKING TO AN ITINERARY

If your permit designates a specific site, and only that site, and you camp somewhere else, you are often liable to a fine. The rangers do, indeed, wander about out there. But they are fair. If you simply could not physically make it, or dark came, or there was some emergency, nobody will fine you. It can happen, whether you work out your route by mail, phone, or in person, that a clerk behind the permit desk will devise a trip that is simply harder than you're used to. Since most of them can hike 20 miles a day without giving it a thought they *can* miscalculate another's abilities. But if you've insisted that a 20-mile hike with a 45-pound pack over several 13,000-foot passes is just what you're used to back there in Springfield, Ohio, and that although you haven't had much time to hike in the past two years you're still in great shape—and if the person at the permit desk issues you a permit accordingly and you don't make your campsite, the ranger may give you a fine. When working out an itinerary, be honest about your ability, with yourself and with the person filling out the permit. Have you been backpacking recently? Consider where you are. Are you used to this kind of terrain? Altitude?

ON YOUR OWN

In a region where there is no such thing as a ranger station or visitor center (in National Forests where backcountry permits are not required, district ranger offices can be far from the area of your hike), you might try to find out something about trails at the best-stocked backpacking store, or at least inquire there who in town knows the trails, then take everything told you with a grain of salt. In National Parks or in Wilderness Areas of National Forests, the rangers check the trails. In other regions you may be about to embark on a hike no one else has made in twenty years.

If you've mapped out your itinerary in advance, you can order, ahead of time, the proper topo maps and whatever guidebooks are available from the visitor center. Or you can purchase them on the spot at the visitor center or a local shop.

Regardless of helpful rangers, maps, and guidebooks, it is never until the end of a trip, after days spent in the backcountry when I have gained some slight familiarity with the particular place, that I feel I can even begin to choose my hike. People, after all, spend whole lifetimes getting to know some relatively small area of wilderness. Ideally one ought to allow enough time to have several days to backpack in the area and then, deliberately, choose one's hike.

4 Weather

Unpredictable. Brilliant clear skies in the rain forests of the Northwest, weeks of hail in the sunny Rockies—anything can happen almost anywhere. Of course, there are patterns: the Northwest and the Smokies are supposed to be the two wettest regions in America. The Northeast also has a certain reputation for dampness. The California mountains are sunny and dry, and the Rockies have clear, brilliant days and nights, with a brief afternoon thundershower. The altitudes in the West make for cold nights, however hot the days, and for cold winds over high passes even on the hottest days. The Mount Washington area in New Hampshire's Presidential Range has the "worst weather in the world." (That's a direct quote from one of their warning signs.) The treeless, beautiful 6,288-foot Mount Washington lays claim to the highest winds ever clocked (231 mph on April 12, 1934), and dense, damp fog rolls in and out of the Presidential Range all the time. Isle Royale, heir to all the vagaries of weather on a Great Lake, can be fogbound, humid, damp—or brilliantly clear and hot. Unless you are hiking in a desert, or possibly in California, you should be prepared even in the height of summer for wet weather and, at high altitudes, for cold nights as well.

SEASONS

Certainly the time of the year *when* you hike has a bearing on the weather. The Sierras and the Rockies are generally clear of snow (where they are ever clear of snow) from mid-July to October. But last winter's snow *could* still be on the ground at the end of July, or next winter's arrive in August. In those areas you are most likely to find the best weather (and the smallest crowds) in September. But if you're interested in wild flowers, you must go toward the end of July. May is a beautiful and relatively cool month in the Smokies, where summer days can be very hot. (May and June are the prime flower months there.) But the beginning of July can still produce snow-hidden trails at elevations lower than the Smokies in the more northern Olympic Peninsula. Altitudes are fairly similar in both places, averaging about 6,000 feet in the Smokies and ranging from 3,000 to 7,954 feet in the Olympics. Yet at 6,642 feet, Clingmans Dome, the highest mountain in the Smokies, is tree-covered, green, and lush; while in the Olympics, altitudes of 5,000 feet are already in the treeless Arctic-Alpine zone. Mount Olympus, at 7,954 feet, just a little more than 1,300 feet higher than Clingmans Dome, possesses seven glaciers.

It's all a matter of life zones—regions dependent on both latitude and altitude where there exists a uniform type of plant and animal life and a single type of climate. The number of life zones varies according to which natural scientist you read, but basically there are six: Lower Sonoran, Upper Sonoran, Transition, Canadian, Hudsonian, and Arctic-Alpine. As an example of how they work—that treeless Arctic-Alpine zone which begins at 5,000 feet in the Olympics would not begin in the Smokies until 10,000 feet. In this hemisphere, every rise in altitude of 1,000 feet equals traveling 200 miles closer to the North Pole. If you are al-

Snow and wildflowers

ready 200 miles closer to the North Pole, you must figure the effects of your 1,000-foot rise into that. You will find certain vegetation at one altitude that does not exist at another. Or, if two altitudes are the same but the latitudes different, you will find certain plants in one place and not in another.

Seasons, too, differ from one altitude and one latitude to another. You could spend a season in the Rockies and never come to summer but simply go from winter to spring to fall, or you could spend a spring in the Smokies and feel yourself in the midst of a lush and flowering summer. Mountain hiking allows you to rearrange time so that summers become endless, open-ended, about to happen, continually about to happen. . . .

WHERE TO GET INFORMATION
ABOUT WEATHER

For up-to-the-minute, accurate information about weather and trail conditions in any area, you should telephone that area. The generalities in the beginning of this chapter must remain, eternally, generalities. If you live in New York City, it is possible to call a number [(212) 399-5561] for the National Weather Service and receive a five-day weather forecast for any area in the U.S. But that is just a forecast, and if in June, wherever you live, you would like some idea of whether trails in the Tetons will be clear enough of snow in mid-July to plan a tour there, you can only really find out by calling the Tetons. Every area can give you expected conditions based on current conditions.

Following are numbers to call for areas described in this book. Since telephone numbers often change, information for anywhere is the area code plus 555-1212.

Olympic National Park—call the Visitor Center, Port Angeles, Washington: (206) 452-9235.

Yosemite National Park—call a special recorded park number for weather and road conditions: (209) 372-4222.

Uncompahgre National Forest—call the District Forest Ranger in Norwood, Colorado: (303) 327-4343.

Grand Teton National Park—call the Visitor Center, Moose, Wyoming: (307) 733-2880.

Isle Royale National Park—call Park Headquarters, Houghton, Michigan: (906) 482-3310.

Great Smoky Mountains National Park—call Park Headquarters, Gatlinburg, Tennessee: (615) 436-5615.

White Mountain National Forest—call the Forest Supervisor, Laconia, New Hampshire: (603) 524-6450.

5 From trails to campsites

Most of the hikes described in this book happen on well-maintained trails. Trails through National Parks and Wilderness Areas of National Forests are generally clear and cared for by the service responsible for them. Abandoned trails sometimes have signs to that effect, but sometimes the discovery is all yours. And walking them can be hard work. I followed one long-unused trail in Colorado. For half a mile, every third step involved climbing up and over a large, limb-wreathed, blown-down tree. It might have been fun without a heavy backpack. Abandoned trails can be hidden by a tangled mass of vegetation or may pass through meadows that have so thoroughly reclaimed them that you get not the slightest hint of where the trails might have gone. Unless you can use a map and compass, avoid abandoned trails.

TRAIL MARKINGS

Maintained trails are easily identifiable both from signs and from obvious use. Where they pass over rocky areas they are usually marked by small piles of stones (cairns or ducks). Occasionally

Trail marker

you may find a trail marked with paint slashes or blazes cut in trees or wooden pickets. Trail intersections are signed. Sometimes, as in Yosemite, it might be hard to find the sign or to figure out which direction it means you to follow. Check your map if you are confused. By 1979, trail signs in all National Parks are supposed to be replaced by standard, easy-to-read signs.

Trail maintenance, even where it is generally good, is not always consistent. In Olympic National Park, for instance, some trails have drainage ditches alongside to keep them from being washed away in storms. (And incidentally, keep your feet much drier.) But, in the same park, occasional other trails seem to disappear in the confusion of a stream crossing or, undrained, lie so much under water in a wet time that you can easily wander off them. Use your map and trust your instinct. You will usually get back on the trail soon again if you have gone in the right direction.

WATERWAYS

Where trails are well maintained, you will usually find bridges over waterways too wide or deep to ford easily. Some parks have lovely wooden bridges across streams, others have unfortunate iron ones. Sometimes the bridges are simply huge trees hauled into position over the water. Occasionally a handrail has been added or the top has been planed off to make a level walkway or wire mesh put over some slippery part of it to keep your foot from slipping.

On those logs without handrails, you may feel, as I do, that there is no possibility of getting across the raging, rolling torrent beneath the log, that your pack *must* unbalance you and pull you in, that even if you didn't have your pack you would be toppled over by mere fate. Stop for an instant, gather yourself together,

Bridge

and simply walk across. Do not hesitate and do not look at the water. Keep your eyes on the log and place your feet evenly one ahead of the other and you will suddenly find yourself across. You will not fall in. Hardly anybody ever falls in.

But just in case, you can be prepared—unbuckle the hip belt of your pack whenever you cross water. This will allow you to wriggle free of your pack if you should fall in, rather than be held down in the water by it.

In crossing streams where there is neither bridge nor stepping-stones within reach of your stride, take off your socks to keep them dry and put your shoes back on. Find yourself a strong enough, long enough stick to brace against the current and walk quickly across with as wide a stride as possible. Your shoes will protect you from sliding on slippery rocks under the water or being pierced by sharp ones and from the numbing effects of icy water. Even if you must walk through fairly deep water, you will not be in it long enough for your boots to actually get waterlogged. Whatever water might seep in will be quickly absorbed by the dry socks you may now put on again. But if your socks get wet, you are asking for blisters.

Do not rearrange the world by building a bridge of any sort. Other people have been getting across without it—why shouldn't you?

Don't minimize the power of rapidly moving water. If you come to white water or areas above waterfalls, continue along the stream until you reach another, calmer place. When snow is melting, stream crossings are at their most dangerous. Water is highest in the late afternoon and early evening so, where possible, cross streams in the morning hours. (That's what you're supposed to do. In fact, you can cross a stream *only* when you come to it.)

If you come to a snow bridge across water, do not use it to cross the stream. Snow next to water, rocks, and logs melts before other snow, and that bridge may break under your weight. Another word about snow: snowfields are icy in the early morning, but they are usually soft and easy to cross once the sun gets to them.

TIMES AND TERRAIN

Weather, snow, and water conditions will influence the time it takes you to make any hike as much as the amount of up and down of the terrain. An easy hike on a sunny day at the end of August can be treacherous and difficult at the beginning of July. Very strong hikers will go faster than the times given at the beginning of each hike in this book, but many people will take more time. An average speed for backpackers is about 2 miles an hour, and I find I am fairly consistently average. It doesn't seem to matter whether the terrain is level or up and down. While I may dawdle on level ground, I tend to walk up most mountains without stopping, since starting again after a stop on the way uphill seems out of the question. In Uncompahgre in the Colorado Rockies, my time was slower than that average. The trails seemed to me no more steep than many in New Hampshire's White Mountains, but they were longer, I was at a higher altitude than usual, and the weather was abominable. In all cases in Part Two I've given *my* time, but included mileage so you can approximate your time based on miles and terrain.

Of all these tours I would say that hiking in the White Mountains was the most consistently difficult (steep ups and downs over rocky, pebbly trails, many of them simply dried-up watercourses) and that only the hikes up over the Rock of Ages Pass in Uncompahgre and the Paintbrush Divide in the Tetons (both involving snow) were more difficult hiking. The rest is generally gentle and presents no problems to anyone used to mountain hiking. Backpackers who have never tried mountains can try any of these, just allowing enough time to acclimate to altitudes and keeping in mind both the vagaries of mountain weather and the fact that mountains *do* go up and down. (Even so, on every route there are level trails.) The nonmountainous Isle Royale is included because it provides some of the most interesting hiking in the Midwest and some of the most diverse and fascinating wildlife anywhere. Hikers not keen on mountains will find a varied landscape there.

LOST?

It is fairly difficult to get lost when hiking on marked trails. It is not, however, impossible to get off on a wrong trail. A sign may not be clear, there may be no sign, you may be distracted by a passing moose, a sudden clap of thunder, or some lovely day-dream. Trail junctions are easy places for the members of a group to lose each other. The faster hikers arrive at the junction first and go ahead in one direction, assuming the direction is obvious. When the slower hikers arrive, they may take another way. Wait at the junction.

If, early on, you feel you have taken a wrong turn and a wrong trail, go back the way you came until you reach your original trail, until you find some familiar place, or until you establish that you have, in fact, been on the right trail all along. If you have gone some distance before realizing you are wrong, or if you have somehow wandered off the trail, stop, sit down, rest, have a drink, check your map. You may be a little misplaced, but you're probably not really lost. Look around you. A topo map will allow you to identify points on the landscape and help you figure out where you're looking at them from. If you've merely gotten off on a wrong trail and can identify the trail you've mistakenly taken, you may find it shorter to proceed the way you are headed to your goal rather than to return and pick up the right trail. But figure it out. While going back can be demoralizing, pressing on may be wrong. Even if the end point is the same, the trail ahead may be long or go over rough terrain you're not used to. Heading cross-country back to your original route is only for people who can use a map and compass. Otherwise you risk turning a perhaps tiring mistake into really getting lost.

If you've gotten off the trail entirely, can you figure out how you got to where you are? Do you see familiar peaks, watercourses, rocks? Can you follow any of these things back to where you used to be on the trail? If not, is there something to climb, a tree or a hill, where you can get a broader view of the landscape? Is there something familiar in the distance you can aim for? Have you worked out some sort of whistle or call that your companions might hear and recognize?

Should any of this happen when darkness is on its way, select a sheltered spot to camp, gather firewood, clear an area down to mineral soil—sand, gravel, or rock—and build yourself a fire. (Vegetable soil—roots, needles, stumps, etc.—can carry a fire underground where it can smolder until sometime later on when it will once again make its way to the surface and be fanned into flame by the wind.) Just the process of tending a fire is enough to keep your mind off being lost. Besides, a fire is cheering. You can work everything else out in the morning.

The Forest Service pamphlet "Outdoor Safety Tips" (PA–887; 15¢) contains everything you need to know about getting lost and surviving. You might find it a useful addition to your first-aid kit.

SIGNAL FOR HELP

If you are injured and alone, stay where you are and build a signal fire. Green boughs or wet leaves create heavy smoke, and any ranger who spots it will come to investigate. The recognized call for help in the mountains is *three signals of any kind, visible or audible* (three regulated puffs of smoke, flashes from a mirror or flashlight, blasts on a whistle, etc.). It should be repeated at regular intervals. When it is recognized, it will be answered by two signals.

CAMPSITES

At the end of your trail is a perfect campsite. Maybe. Whether you are camping in a designated site or not, you must look for the same things: dry, level ground and water are probably the two most important considerations. But don't pitch the tent right next

A perfect campsite

to the water. A heavy rain can turn what seemed like dry ground into a swamp. (Besides, it's usually illegal not to be a certain number of feet from a stream.) Any sort of gully, ravine, or canyon, no matter how protected and inviting it looks, can turn into a watercourse in a storm. Stay out of such places. A hill or woods behind the tent can serve as a windbreak, but don't set up camp under a rockslide slope. High promontories, which may seem magnificent campsites, can be extremely windy and cold. Open meadows, which seem sunny and marvelous when you pitch your tent, will be damp, dew-drenched places by the time you wake up, and if you're in morning shade, the tent will probably not dry out by the time you're ready to pack it up. Then, too, if you're the highest thing around you become a good lightning attractor. If you camp under the only tree in sight, however, or even under a few tall trees, you have then set up camp *beneath* lightning attractors. A stand of pines at the western edge of a remote, sunny meadow with a beautiful clear stream will provide you with a wind-break, lightning detractor, morning sun, and running water . . . indeed the perfect campsite.

If you have a choice, don't camp directly next to, or in view of, somebody else. At some of the more popular campsites on Isle Royale you may find yourself having to ask to *share* a campsite. Ask. You've got to sleep somewhere.

At designated campsites you will often find an outhouse. Under other conditions, find a proper spot 50 to 100 feet away from any open water. Dig (or kick) a hole 8 to 10 inches in diameter and 5 to 8 inches deep. After use, fill the hole with soil.

DRINKING WATER

Water is readily available at almost every campsite mentioned in the trips that follow. Only twice (in Uncompahgre and Isle Royale) was it not. Both times were the first overnights of the respective hike, and water enough for night and morning could be carried from the starting point. A water source was encountered early the next day. On one hike, in the Smokies, it was necessary to backtrack after reaching camp to collect water. But in all these mountains there is no dearth of clear and beautiful water, and it is possible any number of times during most days to refill canteens, often with spring water. On no hike was there ever a day when water was a problem.

Except for spring water (water coming out of the ground), all water should probably be purified with halazone or iodine tablets or boiled. Water on Isle Royale *must* be boiled. Neither water purifiers nor filters work on the hydatid cysts that live in it (see pp. 171–72). In high mountains, above campgrounds, you are probably safe drinking directly from streams. There *could* be a dead sheep or bird or something lying in the stream above you, but you might be willing to take that chance. My feeling is that almost anything is better than the taste of water purifiers.

SOME PROHIBITIONS

In many backcountry areas you may not build a fire, but must use a stove. In other areas, to build a fire you must camp at a fire-site—an area that already has a fire pit or circle. Use the existing fire pit rather than build a new one, although since forests and fire builders are not on a coordinated schedule, you may run into a lack of wood at designated firesites. Your route is always more flexible if you carry and use a stove, and, at times, with a stove you are free to camp anywhere, so long as you meet the region's requirements: at least so many miles from any road; so many feet from a trail, lake, or stream; sometimes so many feet from a shelter. Pack and saddle animals must in some areas be tethered so many feet from a stream. The numbers of feet and miles from various things vary from place to place and often from year to year. Check on it *before* a ranger turns up after you've climbed into your tent for the night and the sun has set, and tells you to move.

Wherever you are, whether permits are required or not, there are some old camping tricks that are no longer practiced, such as trenching around the tent, cutting boughs for beds or shelters, cutting standing trees, dead or alive, and constructing new fire rings where old ones exist. Don't wash in streams or lakes. Use a pot to wash dishes and/or yourself, and throw the soapy water at least 100 feet from the water source. Biodegradable soap pollutes, too. Stroganoff à la suds for dinner (because the people at the next campsite up-river did a bit of washing) is a bit unappetizing.

GARBAGE

Which brings us to garbage. Everybody knows these days that unused food and everything that won't burn (which includes a lot of wrappings for instant food and drink that appear to be paper but are often actually foil-lined and unburnable) must be carried out. For some reason, not everybody does it. Some National Parks have even taken to handing out garbage bags along with back-country permits. Attractive as the bags often are, they should be used for garbage. Not only is garbage exceedingly ugly to come upon, but it creates an artificial food source for animals, which alters their behavior to such an extent that many of them no longer seek their own food and therefore starve to death in the winter. It is, by the way, chiefly for that reason you should never feed any wild animal.

6 A certain amount about what you need

Your feet should work properly. Good, broken-in boots matter more than anything else. If you are planning a backpacking trip and need new boots, put the trip off long enough to wear the boots awhile. You should not be frugal when buying boots, although you won't necessarily need the most expensive. Often a cheaper boot will fit *your* foot better. A lightweight trail shoe that is immediately comfortable, or very easy to break in, is ideal for gentle trails with a light pack, but it won't do for backpacking. You need a stiffer boot with wider soles which help distribute the weight of a heavy pack and a stiffer sole reinforced by a midsole which helps protect your feet from sharp rocks. You do *not* want the very stiff, full shank (of metal, wood, or plastic) mountaineering boot.

How do you know if they fit? With the boot unlaced and your toes touching the front of the boot, you should be able to get your finger between your heel and the boot's heel. When the boot is tightly laced, your heel should be lodged firmly in the heel cup and you should not be able to lift it more than ⅛ inch. It should fit snugly around the ball of your foot so that your foot cannot move around on its own inside the boot. And your toes should not hit the end of the boot when you tap your foot (toe first) into the floor (or while descending steep terrain). Try the boot on with the sock or socks you will wear hiking.

Once you've got your boots home you should, before wearing them, rub them with an oil-base treatment if they've been oil-tanned, or if they've been chrome-tanned (most boots are), rub them with a silicone- or wax-base treatment like Sno-Seal, a wax-and-silicone mixture. For the welt and midsoles of *all* boots, use something like Leath-R-Seal (a mixture of shellac, wax, and beeswax), since oil and some of the solvents used in silicone dissolve the cement holding the soles to the boot and weaken the stitching. When you buy the boots, ask what to use on them. You should go through the same process after every trip where they've gotten wet. (*After* they've dried, that is.) Always keep the boots away from excessive heat, which will dry the life out of the leather. Don't dry them in front of the fire, or in the oven, or on the radiator. If they're very wet, stuff them with newspaper and put them in a cool, dry place. If they get wet on the trail, stuff them with a dry sock overnight. If they're still wet in the morning, make sure you have dry socks to wear. If it has stopped raining, they'll dry quickly as you walk. If it hasn't stopped raining, it won't make much difference.

There is a mystique about boots and their care. Mystiques don't interest me a lot. I wore a marvelous pair of boots five full summers in the Alps and a summer and winter in America without ever doing anything more than stuffing them with newspaper when they got wet and they remained marvelous. It was only in their seventh year of wear that they began to leak. Sno-Seal and Leath-R-Seal applied often helped, but at that point it was time to buy new boots. I carefully Sno-Sealed them, of course.

You can protect your feet from blisters in new (or old) boots by applying moleskin to them beneath every pressure point of the boot, before you start out. If you get a blister, cut out a space for the blister from a piece of moleskin and put the moleskin *around* the blister (making sure you've cut out enough so the moleskin does not touch the blister). The moleskin will keep the boot from pressing against the blister. If your toes hurt going down-hill, wrap the whole front of them with lamb's wool, which you can buy in a drugstore. It's what ballet dancers put in their toe shoes—you think *your* toes get knocked about!

RAINGEAR

After boots, the next most important thing is proper raingear. Since it can rain for days at a time and being dry in a cold wind can make a difference between life and death, and since the only way you can be dry while backpacking in the rain is to *stay* dry, it makes sense to invest in good raingear. Rainsuits or a combi-nation of poncho, parka, or cagoule (a full-cut, extra-long pullover parka with a hood—nice because it doesn't billow out like a poncho) with rain chaps or pants all serve the same purpose. A poncho can be used in other ways as well—as ground cloth, emer-gency shelter, pack cover, etc., etc. Many people prefer ponchos since they allow more air to pass through than a more enclosed garment. (Condensation inside waterproof materials often makes the wearer wetter than does the precipitation outside.) All rain-gear is made of lightweight coated nylon. After a while, on some of them, the coating will begin to crack and wear off. Buy another immediately because that one will no longer keep you dry. A test for rainproofness is to blow through the garment. If you can feel breath on your hand, buy something else.

CLOTHES

Wear something comfortable to hike in. Many people wear fairly loose-fitting blue jeans. Other people say blue jeans are impracti-cal since they are cold when it's cold, hot when it's hot, and when they get wet they generally stay wet a long time. But long pants of some sort give you the most protection when walking through thick woods or dense growth or in areas of poison ivy or rattlesnakes. Shorts are comfortable when you're out from under creeping forests, although if you're at a high altitude without the protection of the woods, you should probably not hike in shorts unless your legs are used to being exposed to bright sun and high winds. Knickers, which very few American backpackers wear, but which everybody wears hiking in Europe, still seem to me the most practical hiking clothing. If it's hot you push your socks down, if it's cold you pull them up, and knickers do not bind no matter how you move your legs.

If you're not used to strong sun, a long-sleeved cotton shirt will keep you cool and protect you from burning rays. If you're used to sun, or are hiking at lower altitudes, T-shirts are comfortable. In cooler weather a lightweight wool shirt is comfortable. Just make sure that whatever you're wearing next to your skin is a natural fiber—wool and cotton are more moisture-absorbent than synthetics and cause you to perspire less. Wool stays warm even if it gets wet. Synthetics are more water- and wind-repellent.

At high altitudes a wool sweater and down parka are both good to have at night. You may often want one or the other at lower altitudes at night as well, or, early and late in the season, both. At high altitudes long underwear can be nice to sleep in. You may or may not want extra underwear (dark colors might help you think it's cleaner longer), but you must have extra socks. Clean, dry socks help prevent blisters. (For that matter, even dirty, *dry* socks do.) Dry wool socks can make a wet boot bearable. Many people like two pair of socks, a thin wool liner with a heavier wool sock over it. Wool absorbs the moisture from your foot, keeping it warmer in cold weather, cooler in warm. With two pair of socks the friction (which is what causes blisters) is between your socks rather than between sock and boot. For high altitudes, throw into your pack a wool hat and gloves, a brimmed hat for the sun, and sunglasses for the snow. A bandanna is a good thing to have

—you can wrap it around your head, use it for a handkerchief, a washcloth, a sling, etc. And don't forget camp shoes—sneakers, moccasins, down booties—something so you can get out of your boots.

HOUSE AND HOME

A down sleeping bag will make you happiest (warmest, lightest to carry) at high altitudes, but for summer backpacking at lower altitudes where you want less warmth, a lightweight synthetic may be even more comfortable. If you use a down bag you need a pad—ensolite, foam, or air mattress—to put under it. Some people have begun sleeping in hammocks in order to reduce body impact on the earth. Hammocks, of course, require trees.

In the drier West, many people carry no form of shelter, but generally it makes sense to carry a tent or a tarp. Carry a stove, and fuel for it, everywhere. Even if fires are allowed, you may not find enough dry wood. In some places where there is little deadfall left, it may be specifically forbidden to pick it up. Besides, stoves are fast and clean—dinner in a hurry and no blackened pots to carry around with you.

Take cooking utensils (i.e., at least one pot in which to boil water), a bowl to eat from (you can eat dinner as well as soup and cereal, etc., from a bowl), and a cup that will keep liquids hot without burning your lips. (Sierra Club cups of tempered metal are designed to do that; there are copies that cost as much but are not tempered in the same way. There are also plastic cups that work as well.) And you need cutlery. You can probably manage with just a spoon if you're eating freeze-dried or finger foods. If you're planning on fishing, you'll need a fork. If you own one of those lightweight cutlery sets that you can buy at every back-packing store, leave the knife at home and carry instead a sharp knife, jackknife, or hunting knife. The knife with the set is just extra weight. Take some sort of scrubber to wash pots and dishes with. Be sure to heat enough water at dinner to use for washing afterward.

FOOD

Check out the stock of freeze-dried foods in your backpacking store or order them by mail if there's no store near you (addresses in Appendix F) or put together your own dry foods from the supermarket. Freeze-dried food is not cheap (but it's no more expensive than going out for a hamburger and milk shake in most places). Some of it is better than others. "Better" means: more taste and tenderness, less water necessary. It also usually means a bit more money. My own preference, after having eaten almost everything in sight, is for Mountain House brand, but I also use a lot of ordinary instant things (soups, oatmeal, pudding, etc.) from the supermarket.

If you make freeze-dried food in its own packages, you never have to wash a pot. There are, of course, people devoted to eating magnificently on a backpacking trip. I know one man who often hikes with a friend who used to be a chef at the Plaza Hotel in New York. They don't walk very far, but they certainly eat well. And when I've camped near somebody with a sizzling pan of fresh fish on his fire, I wonder whether the efficiency of freeze-dried food is really worth it. But the fact is that all my elegant tastes seem to leave me the minute I'm faced with having to clean up the mess elegance inevitably leaves on a camping trip. Besides, I *like* chili mac with beans.

OTHER GEAR

Take a gallon, or larger, collapsible water jug for use in camp, one or two quart or liter and/or pint canteens, preferably wide-mouthed to use on the trail where the pint is often handy for mixing lunch drinkables; a small lightweight grill (backpacking stores); a flashlight; waterproof matches or matches in a waterproof case (make sure they strike on whatever you have to strike them on); insect repellent; sun cream or antisun cream; a first-aid kit and a snakebite kit; toilet paper; extra plastic bags for garbage, laundry, etc.; thread (not a whole sewing kit—wrap a good length of thread around a needle); a metal mirror, which can be used for reasons of vanity or for signaling; a lightweight plastic ground cloth to put under your tent, or in your tent under your sleeping bag, or under your sleeping bag on the ground; salt tablets; halazone or other water purifiers; a waterproof stuff sack large enough to hold *all* your food to hoist up into a tree at night; nylon cord (50 feet, 550-pound test weight, ⅛-inch diameter) for tying up the food sack and a hundred other things; an extra ground cloth or poncho or space blanket to rig a shelter to cook and eat under in a rainstorm—carefully placed so that it doesn't immediately ignite. And don't forget compass, appropriate maps, guidebooks, and a copy of *Mountaineering Medicine* by Fred T. Darvill, Jr., M.D. This small wilderness medical guide, designed to carry in your pack, is available from the Skagit Mountain Rescue Unit, P.O. Box 2, Mt. Vernon, Washington 98273, for $1.00. The dollar goes to aid the local (Mt. Vernon) mountain rescue unit.

In the category of extra weight, but possibly handy, are a whistle for signaling, something wonderful to read, and/or some miniature game if you like to have something to do at the end of the day. If you play it extremely well, you might take along a harmonica.

A perfectly wonderful thing to carry on a backpacking trip, which has not yet been invented, would be a compressed water tablet. If sprinkled with a few drops of water in a large container, it would immediately dissolve, expand, and fill the entire container with water. Ideally it would be compressed of pure, high Rocky Mountain water.

7 Cars, buses, thumbs, boats, cable cars, and mules

CARS AND BUSES

America is based on the premise that each inhabitant has his own car. Nothing, therefore, is central. Why, for instance, is there not a National Park or Forest visitor center or ranger station located in the gateway towns to the parks, the towns to which one might be able to arrive by bus or plane or even train? It is usually necessary to travel some distance to it, and once there, you may still have a number of miles to go to the start of your hike. The route to the visitor center is rarely serviced by public transportation.

Although there are many problems caused by its overdevelopment, Yosemite Valley is still a great and rare example of a tourist area equipped to deal with something besides the material needs (food, lodging, souvenirs) of tourists. A free shuttle bus travels three separate loops in the valley every 10 to 15 minutes. You can transfer from one loop to another, so there is no place in the valley you cannot reach. There is also a special service for hikers (and others) that provides transportation from the valley up to the high country. You can, for instance, take the bus up to Tuolumne Meadows (just one of many stops) for $5.50 (as of this writing), or for less to any point before the Meadows. You could travel from San Francisco, Fresno, or Merced on public transportation, take the bus up to Tuolumne Meadows where there is a ranger station, hike for as long as you like, and either hike or take the bus back down to the valley and a bus back to your starting point. A leader in the formation of National Parks, Yosemite is also a leader in making them truly accessible without, at the same time, encouraging even more cars. Eventually, depending on the outcome of a new master plan for the park (see pp. 114–15), all auto traffic may be banned from the valley.

Ideally, auto traffic should be banned from all parks. And,

Bus stop in the Tetons

in fact, recommendations to that effect were made by the Washington-based Conservation Foundation's 1972 Symposium on the National Parks of the Future (held in Yosemite) to do everything possible to separate the park visitor from his car. Leaving his car or "motor home" at the park's edge, the visitor should then be able to travel in the park via public transportation, be it bus or rail. The Symposium even envisioned a system of public transportation from the major cities to the parks. The question, of course, is, when *is* the future?

In the Smokies a private shuttle service provides a civilized means of getting to and from your hike.

To reach Isle Royale you can make use of once-a-day Greyhound bus service from Duluth to Grand Portage, overnight there, and take the boat in the morning. You must also overnight in Grand Portage on your return, since the return bus to Duluth leaves too early in the morning for the boat to connect with it.

There is a sort of sporadic bus in the Tetons that travels back and forth between Jackson Lake Lodge, the airport, and Jackson that can cut out the necessity for some hitching.

HITCHING

Hitching. That's the whole point. If every American is expected to have one car, every hiker must have two, or be content to work out a lifetime of circular routes, or, often in middle age, take up hitching. Part of what I like about hiking is going from one place to another, which probably stems from having missed some Ohio to California trek in 1845. I've no great pleasure in ending up where I began. But under those circumstances, unless I am willing to hitch, I must have a car to get me to my starting point and another waiting at the end. But I also dislike having to travel to the end before arriving at the start. Therefore, although it is not my first choice of a way to travel, there is usually no choice *but* to hitchhike. I cannot keep from taking it personally when a car with room in it passes without stopping, even though I understand the fear people have of hitchhikers. The sight of a backpack alleviates some of that fear, but then lots of people don't stop because I *am* a backpacker and therefore dusty while their car isn't. Nevertheless, I've never had to wait *very* long, or walk *many* miles, before getting a ride.

I'm enormously appreciative of those people who do stop, all of whom seem genuinely friendly and invariably interesting (like the people in second-class cars on European trains). Almost everyone who has ever given me a ride has gone out of his way to leave me off where I was going instead of where he was going. One car had a guest book. A brother and sister driving across the country had deliberately sought out hitchhikers, and their book carried the names of people from all over America and half of Europe. Many of the people who have stopped for me are hikers themselves, but not all of them. Nor do they fall into any particular age category. The only real thing they have in common is that they're nice people.

All of which is to say that any of you who have never hitched need not, in hiking country, fear it. While traditionally a male/female couple has the easiest time getting a ride, it is as acceptable for a woman alone or two women together to hitch as it is for men. Most drivers who do stop will probably see those figures by the road first as backpackers or hikers. In recognition of the impossibility of public transportation, most states generally allow hitching on secondary roads as long as you stand off the pavement. Even where it is not precisely legal, the local police are usually both tolerant and helpful. Obviously two people hitching will more easily get a ride than a larger group. Backpacks take up a lot of space. Families will do better by temporarily splitting up—unless they prefer to wait for someone with an empty van to arrive. Trailer drivers, unlike van drivers, probably won't be of help. No one in a trailer has ever offered me a ride, although many trailers pass with spare tires encased in canvas decorated with a smiling face.

BOATS, CABLE CARS, AND MULES

There are areas in a number of National Parks, such as parts of Everglades National Park in Florida or parts of the Ross Lake and Lake Chelan National Recreational Areas, contiguous with North Cascades National Park in Washington, that can be reached only by boat or plane. In Lake Chelan there is a shuttle bus connecting with the boat. Isle Royale is our only entirely roadless National Park, so one *must* reach it by either boat or plane. Anyplace that can be reached by means other than car (or plane) automatically has an appeal for me.

Hiking the summer trails bordering on most large ski areas offers the possibility of beginning your hike with a ride up the mountain via cable car, gondola, or chair lift. Some people think this is cheating, but I think it's nice. Of the hikes described in the book, two offer that possibility. In the Tetons you can ride the cable car up to the top of Rendezvous Mountain, saving you 4,000 feet in some long, steep miles of uphill. Or in the White Mountains you may ride the gondola up to the top of Wildcat, saving you about 2,000 feet in about 2½ miles of uphill.

You may also use one variety of transportation *instead* of hiking. In many areas of the U.S. (and along most of the routes described) you may travel by horse or, particularly in Yosemite, by mule. A list of packers is in Appendix D.

8 How to deal with a moose and other survival matters

"What about bears?" I asked.

"Oh, you'll never see one up there," the ranger answered. "Anyway, a bear will keep out of your way. It's the moose you've got to worry about. They're the dangerous ones. Ornery, you know . . . moose . . ."

I was camped in a perfectly splendid clearing in a stand of pines, the floor flat and soft with endless years of pine needles, the edges of the clearing furnished with huge fallen logs to sit on or lean against. The clearing was set back from the path, and the path led to a spring whose pure and cold water rushed down out of the earth and over rocks to join the river a few hundred yards downhill.

I arrived in the midafternoon, set up camp, and went to spend the remainder of the day on a sun-hot rock above the river where it flowed near the path higher up. The water plunged and foamed and roared its way down from the glacier still higher. When the sun left my rock I returned to the clearing, heated water on the stove for dinner, ate with a great contentment, sipped a bit of brandy, and crawled into my tent.

It was a little past 7:00 and darker in the clearing than on the path, but still light enough to read. I had been reading about twenty minutes when I heard a sound behind the tent. I am always alert to sounds, but once in my tent I try to ignore them. As I lay there, rigidly ignoring this one, I heard it again, the sound of a large movement. I looked out the back window. A bull moose stood a foot behind the tent, his head slightly lowered, eyeing this object in his path.

"It's the moose you've got to worry about," I heard the ranger saying. Well, yes, and this one seemed rather close. Of course, they're nearsighted so I supposed he had to come close to see the tent. On the other hand, if he had come close because the tent was pitched in his path, perhaps he would ignore the tent, that is, walk over it. Or perhaps he would quite deliberately get it out of his way.

"Hello, Moose," I said. "Nice evening." (I picked up the habit of talking to things that frightened me when first faced with what seemed angry and definitely horned cows in my path in the Alps. I think they thought it was their path.) The moose looked confused and backed away a few steps. I suppose he hadn't expected a tent that talked.

"You certainly are a beautiful color," I continued. He was. Even as I awaited imminent trampling under his hooves, I was aware he was a handsome beast, with a rich, beautiful coat, not at all like those ugly heads mounted on the walls of bars. Slowly he picked his way around the tree to the right of the tent, crossed the clearing, crossed the path, and ran down through the woods toward the river.

So, I had survived my first encounter with a moose. But wouldn't he come back? Wasn't this his route home? Down to the river for a drink and some dinner and then home? But, after all, he had only been curious, confused, frightened. Any wild animal is frightened by man. And while I'm certain the fear I felt/feel is no different from the animal's fear—it is, after all, born of the same instinct—its initiation in me is followed by all the rational knowledge I've ever acquired, i.e., the animal is afraid, he may react in certain ways, I must act in certain ways neither to frighten him further nor to anger him. I'm not at all sure the animal isn't better off without going through all that; ultimately less frightened, since he simply acts on his fear while I manage to build up such a wealth of possibilities that I certainly compound mine.

In any case, as I sat there groping with a final analysis of fear, I heard a rustling to the left of the tent, toward the front of it. I looked out the front, and there, at the edge of the clearing, still half in the trees, stood the cow, staring at the tent. As I watched she came out of the trees, edged along the side of them, giving a distinct impression of being on tiptoe, reached the path, and bounded down through the woods to join the bull. I did not think at all then. I merely packed up my sleeping bag, took down the tent, retrieved the food sack from its tree, loaded my pack, and left. It was 7:30 when the cow appeared. At 7:50 I was on the path, headed downhill.

The sun was gone but the light remained in the sky. Toward the west the sky was streaked with red. I was about two miles up the mountain and about three from a lodge in the valley. It was a very expensive lodge, but money no longer mattered. I had one hour until it was totally dark. It was a time of no moon. I heard a crashing sound on my left and could just make out two elk bounding away through the woods. The sky became grayer, the red streaks brighter. I entered deep woods and lost most of the light, came out of them again to what seemed, in contrast, brilliant light. I heard more crashing in the woods on my left, but this time saw nothing.

I reached the bottom of the mountain as the last light left the sky. A large herd of grazing animals stood dim and hulking against the dark. They were probably elk, but in the wide, vast valley where nothing existed except shapes, I had somehow arrived on the African veldt. Zebra no doubt, or eland. The first stars were hidden under thin clouds. I crossed the plain on the path I could barely make out beneath my feet, led on now by the light from the lodge at the far end.

Through the window I could see elegant people lingering over coffee and liqueur, while others now strolled out onto the porch for the night air. I leaned my pack against the building and entered.

"May I help you?" the clerk asked.

"I'd like a room for tonight," I answered, assuming as much haughtiness as possible in compensation for my attire, which I had now worn four days in the backcountry. It had also been some time since I had combed my hair.

"Madam, this is August," the clerk announced. The people in the lobby turned to look at me.

"Well, what do you suggest then?" I stood a bit taller. The trick, obviously, was to make him think he had done something wrong.

"There *is* another lodge about twelve miles down the road, but I'm sure *they're* full."

"Then what else? I'm traveling by foot." The people in the lobby turned away from me.

"I'm sure *I* don't know. You might try sleeping by the road."

"Yes," I said. "I might."

I returned to the meadow. The clouds had rolled back and the stars were near and brilliant. I laid out my sleeping bag beneath a pine tree and had a superb, if illegal, night's sleep.

Later in the summer when I found a moose staring into my tent, I did not move. I was concerned that, with her nearsighted-ness, in the tiny space where I had set the tent she would trip over the ropes. She didn't. She ate some of the bushes around me and went away.

I'm not sure all of that has as much to do with moose as it does with fear. It was misguided (inexperienced) fear. My feeling was, the first time, that I had put my tent in a moose path and

I had better get it off. In fact it was, even at the time, exciting to see a moose so close. But fear is not an unrealistic thing when wandering in the places of wild animals. So long as it serves as a means of keeping you out of their way, fear is a useful thing and no reason to stay out of the backcountry.

Wild animals will almost always take fright at your appearance and run away. Or, in any case, move out of your path. You will never even see most wild animals, although they will, unseen, be watching you.

FEEDING ANIMALS

Some animals have become used to living on handouts from campers. They are no less wild because of it, only in addition to being wild they have become, for the first time, dangerous. An animal used to handouts will be demanding of them. Don't give them anything! The most important reason is, as I mentioned earlier, that feeding them can alter their behavior to the extent that they no longer seek their own food. A second, and perhaps more personal, reason is that all warm-blooded animals can carry diseases like bubonic plague and rabies. A bite from a rabid chipmunk or ground squirrel is as deadly as one from a rabid dog. Any tidbit proffered can result in a bitten finger. It's not worth it, for them or you. I have seen people offering nuts to chipmunks in order to get a photo. I also heard of a man who put honey on his child's face so he could get a picture of a bear licking her.

Bears are neither teddy bears nor large dogs. And in spite of the proliferation of postcards in bear country with pictures of bears eating ice-cream cones and leaning their forepaws cutely against cars, they are wild animals. They are a nuisance only where they have been made a nuisance by sightseers and campers who leave food where they can get it or who deliberately feed them. When they go after what *you* plan to eat, and you want to keep it for yourself, they can become angry.

WHAT TO DO WHEN ANIMALS DO
NOT DISCREETLY DISAPPEAR

If an animal is lying or walking in your path, *you* get out of *its* way. If a moose (or any of the hooved animals) should charge you, either get up a tree or get some trees between you and it. Do not try to outrun it over open ground. You can't. If an animal is not in the process of charging you, do not move suddenly, but talk to it in a reassuring way as you look around for a tree to climb or move slowly out of its world. I don't know for sure what it does for the animal, but the tone should help *you*.

If you encounter a grizzly, climb a tree. This, of course, involves knowing *how* to climb a tree. If you do not know how to climb a tree and you say to people who do, "But I don't know how to climb a tree," they will *always* say, "When you have to, you'll know how." You may or may not find this comforting. (If you do not find this comforting, see pp. 52–53.)

A black bear will usually stay away from you unless you've angered it, but grizzlies are not noted for their rationality. Black bears can climb trees. Adult grizzlies cannot. If you cannot get up a tree, lie on your stomach or on your side with your legs drawn up to your chest, clasp your hands over the back of your neck, and play dead. Grizzlies have simply passed people in this position without hurting them, or at most only slightly injured them by inflicting a few halfhearted slaps. In order to keep things from coming to this point, a little noise can be helpful. Wearing a bell, singing, or hiking with a nonstop talker will let any bears around know you're there. By choice they will stay away. Of course, so will every other animal.

The National Park Service has published a pamphlet "In Grizzly Country." Available at visitor centers in Glacier National Park, it should be required reading before starting a hike in any grizzly country. (In the U.S. outside of Alaska, grizzly country means, generally, the northern Rockies, although there are rumors of a few bears in Colorado's San Juan Mountains.)

All female animals protecting their young are dangerous. And almost any young animal you see along the trail has a watchful mother somewhere nearby who is sure you are out to do her progeny some harm. Think of your own protective instincts about your children or mates or even pets. Do not *ever* go near any young animal. If you see one by itself, get as far from it as you can as quickly as possible. Just being *between* it and its mother will alarm the mother.

Usually any animal who *will* approach you is sick. Sickness makes wild animals less wary of man. The animal may be appealing, but it *is* sick. Don't go near it.

PROTECTING YOUR FOOD

The waterproof sack for your food mentioned earlier is important. At night, or any time you leave a campsite, place *all* food in the sack and hang it from a tree. Choose a strong enough branch about 20 feet above the ground, tie a rock to the free end of the rope attached to the food sack, and throw the rock (and rope) over the branch. Position the sack about 5 feet below the branch, 10 feet from the trunk of the tree, and 15 feet above the ground. Remove the rock and tie off the end of the rope in a small tree some distance from the sack tree. If you tie two pots or metal cups to the outside of the stuff sack, they will rattle if an animal should somehow get to the sack and, hopefully, scare him away. Since black bears can climb trees, the sack must be hung far enough from the trunk so they cannot climb the tree and just reach out for it. Grizzlies, who can be 7 feet tall, can reach up pretty high. There are places where you'll have trouble finding the proper tree. Keep looking.

All the food precautions pertain even when you are not in bear country. Fox, raccoons, mice, and virtually every other creature will get into your food if they can. You should also not leave food in your backpack (although some people hang up their whole packs at night). There isn't much point in having an expensive pack ripped open in this eternal search. There was a bear in the Smokies who collected packs. People would wake in the morning, or leave and then return to a campsite, to find their packs gone. The rangers finally found the bear and her pack cache after one group of hikers reported their packs missing but refused to leave an address in case they were found. The rangers reported that among the goodies in the packs were some large stashes of pot. They had no comment about the bear.

Shelters in the Smokies have been bearproofed; that is, the fronts have been closed off with strong wire fencing and you enter through latched doors. The only problem with the shelters is that they have attracted a large population of mice who seem to prefer living indoors. They run back and forth across the rafters at night and in and out of the packs. A ranger suggested placing ponchos over the packs so the mice couldn't get a foothold, but would just slide down. Food in shelters—anywhere—should be hung from the rafters, too far down for the mice to jump onto. I don't know how far down a mouse can jump, but none ever got into mine, a few feet from the middle of the ceiling.

A FEW SPECIAL PRECAUTIONS

Clean scrupulously all pots and pans, dishes, eating utensils, etc., so they have no food odor left on them, or put them in the food sack, too. If you have cans of any sort, burn them so the food odor is destroyed before consigning them to the garbage sack, which should also be in the food sack. Never, never eat anything at all in your tent or your sleeping bag. Even if you then remove the food, the odor may remain and a bear following the scent will not hesitate to rip into the tent, the bag, or you. It's also best not to sleep in the clothes you wore while cooking and to sleep some

Pika with his own food

distance from your cooking area. Women should stay out of bear country while menstruating, and nobody should wear or carry perfume, hair spray, deodorant, or cosmetics. All these scents have been thought to attract and anger bears.

HOW TO CLIMB A TREE

Look for a tree with branches close to the ground but spaced far enough apart so you can get your body close to the trunk of the tree. This is usually difficult with fir and pine trees. Deciduous trees are the best and, of these, poplars and aspens ideal. Branches need not be long and thick—the smallest beginning of a branch will support your foot. If there is nothing close enough to the ground to put your foot on, look for a branch low enough to be reached with your hands. Grab it and grip the tree trunk with your knees (as if it were a sort of vertical horse). You can grip the trunk with very little pressure since the bark is rough and will help you. Your handhold is not so much to pull yourself up with as it is for balance as you hoist yourself onto the first branch and into a standing position. (Sit on it first if you need to.) Reach up to the next branch using the same technique. The next higher branch may be on the other side of the tree, so you may have to shift around the trunk. If the trunk is not too thick, you can hold on to it. Continue gripping the trunk with your knees and keep your weight close to the trunk as you go from one branch to the next. The branches get thinner as you go higher, so pick branches that will hold your weight. Most will hold your weight at the point at which they grow out of the trunk. Don't step out on the branch, but remain close to the trunk. If it is a small limb (½ inch or so thick), don't put all your weight on it, but let your hands, either on the next branch or on the tree trunk, take some of your weight.

When you are ready to come down, hang on to the trunk or a sturdy limb until your foot is firmly planted on the next lower branch, and so on until you reach the ground.

You might want to practice this at a time when you are not being chased by anything.

HORSES AND MULES

Two other animals that are not wild, but which need mentioning, are horses and mules. They *always* have the right of way on a trail. If you encounter one animal or a whole train of them, move off the path, preferably uphill and in a calm manner. It is not only proper etiquette but also common sense, since a frightened animal can cause a lot of problems, not the least of which can be for you if you happen to be standing in its path.

9 A few dangers
of varying degrees

STORMS

Rain, hail, sleet, snow, wind—anything nature can conjure up—
can come at any time in the high mountains. You should be prepared to survive it all. If a storm is accompanied by lightning,
do not continue hiking upward, get off exposed ridges and peaks,
avoid exposed lone objects like huge boulders or single trees or
isolated buildings, and avoid being the highest object yourself or
taking shelter beneath the highest object. Stay away from all metal
—cables, bridges, fences, etc. Put your pack, ice axe, anything of
the sort, down in one spot and go sit somewhere else, under some
low trees or shrubs or in some low area. If there is absolutely
nowhere to go, squat so that the rubber of your shoes remains on
the ground.

A person hit by lightning can often be revived by a combi-
nation of artificial respiration and heart massage, both of which
are described in *Mountaineering Medicine*.

Once the lightning stops, there is no reason not to hike in the rain unless it is accompanied by fog through which you cannot see. In that case, go down instead of up. If it is hailing, the higher you go the larger the hailstones, so you might also want to remain out of their pelting fury.

HYPOTHERMIA

The prime killer in the mountains and in all the outdoors is hypothermia, which is caused by exposure to cold, aggravated by wet, wind, and exhaustion. It begins with violent shivering, which can develop in air temperatures between 30 and 50 degrees if there is a wind and you have gotten wet. What happens is that your body loses heat faster than it produces it, and your response, both voluntary (exercising to get warm) and involuntary (shivering), drains your energy, a process that can be stopped only by reducing the degree of exposure.

One of the greatest dangers in hypothermia is that a person suffering from it is unaware of it. He must be immediately warmed by ending the exposure or his judgment becomes impaired. He loses control of his hands, speech becomes slow and slurred. He becomes incoherent, stumbling, drowsy as his internal temperature slides down. Without treatment, he will die.

The chief defense against hypothermia is to stay dry. That means putting on proper raingear *before* you get wet and putting on wool clothes *before* you start shivering. See that everybody with you has adequate gear before you start out. Look for the first signs of shivering when anyone in your party has been exposed to cold and wet and get him warm fast. Take him into a warm place; remove all wet clothes; get him into dry, preferably wool clothes and a warm sleeping bag; give him warm drinks. If the person is already only semiconscious, keep him awake, give him warm drinks, and leave him undressed in a sleeping bag with another person, also undressed, or between two warm, undressed people if you have a double bag. Skin-to-skin contact is the most effective treatment.

Most parks distribute a brochure about hypothermia. Read it and carry it with you. Or check *Mountaineering Medicine*.

THIEVES

Thieves are a fact of life. Maybe it's an ultimate socialism where everything is everybody's just for the taking. Whatever it is, there *is* a good deal of taking. Wherever you leave your car, make sure you have nothing left inside it. Everything you are not carrying should be stored in the trunk, and, if possible, do not leave the car in an isolated place.

Thieves vary. They can be local people, passersby, hikers, and bears. If you've left food inside your car, a bear can wreak havoc going after it. In one incident last August, bears ransacked all the cars but one in a Yosemite parking lot. That one had a faulty brake-light switch that kept the taillights flashing on and off for the days the car's owners were hiking. The battery was dead when they got back, but the bears hadn't touched the car. I've already mentioned the Smokies bear who collected packs. In that same Yosemite parking lot, all four wheels had been removed from one car, but not by bears. Yosemite, for example, has a race of hikers devoted to living free. They steal only what they require to maintain themselves in the backcountry—food and equipment, nothing extra.

Whenever you leave a car in an isolated spot, you risk its invasion. At least that's what I've heard, although my luck has been consistently good everywhere. Still, in at least one instance, in the Smokies, that good luck was probably the result of a warning from a ranger to park in one spot rather than in another.

In the Smokies you can further guard against theft by taking advantage of the shuttle arrangement described in the Smokies

chapter. You might be able privately to work out similar arrangements with gas stations or hotels in other areas. Otherwise, where
you can, park in the most public place possible, and where you can't,
you'll have to trust to luck.

ALTITUDE

Altitude affects people differently. Some people it doesn't affect at
all. Others may experience headache, sleeplessness, shortness of
breath, lack of appetite, a general lassitude, bad dreams. Most
women will experience changes in their menstrual cycle, which
can be moved up as much as a week. Such symptoms are caused
by the decreasing amount of oxygen in the air as you go higher.
The altitude at which you experience any of these things is wholly
individual. If you are caused great discomfort, go lower for a day
or two. Allow time to acclimate if you plan to hike in the Sierras
or the Rockies or anywhere high and are used to life at sea level.

TICKS

Of all the various small creatures, I mention only these since
they are, in their way, the most dangerous and are less easily
avoided than snakes, spiders, tarantulas, and scorpions. You can
avoid snakes by not putting your hand on rocks or fallen trees without looking first, and the others by shaking out shoes and clothing
before putting them on and shaking out sleeping bags before getting
in. Scorpion and poisonous spider bites should be treated as you do
snakebites. (See *Mountaineering Medicine* or the instructions in
your snakebite kit.)
    But back to ticks. They exist everywhere, but in some parts
of the West they carry the germs of Rocky Mountain spotted
fever, which can be treated with antibiotics if caught in time, but
which would be best to avoid in the first place. To make sure there

are no ticks embedded in you, a daily check of your entire body is in order. If you find a tick and cannot easily brush it off, apply fuel from your stove to it. Alcohol, kerosene, grease, oil, or nail polish will all make it let go its hold (although why you'd be carrying nail polish is beyond me). When the tick drops off, kill it. Don't try to pull one off. It will leave its head embedded in you and cause infection. As soon as you've killed the tick, clean the bite and apply alcohol or antiseptic to it. A lighted match or cigarette will also make a tick drop off, but as you must hold the fire so near it may burn you, this is recommended only if you have none of the other things available. Use a tick repellent (Off, for instance) in tick-infested areas. If you are going into an area known to contain infected ticks, ask your doctor about immunization.

10 Fishing

In spite of a passion for fish, it has never occurred to me to go and catch one. As I wandered through these various wildernesses, I marveled at the number of people who do. Aside from those who find their way into at least the peripheral backcountry *just* to fish, there are countless others for whom fishing gear is standard equipment on a backpacking trip. The rivers and streams run with piscatorial abundance, and the odor of fish sautéing over well-tended fires at sunset wafts across to such fishless campers as I, utterly dissolving me in envy.

Fishing gear does not take up much space. Reels with collapsible handles and lightweight rods that can be broken down to fit in your pack are generally available. If you can't find them near you, write to Recreational Equipment, Inc., 1525 11th Avenue, Seattle, Washington 98122, for their catalog.

Standard survival equipment, by the way, includes a few fishhooks and a few feet of monofilament fishing line.

When cleaning fish, do not dispose of the entrails near the lake or stream, since they will attract bears who also fish and may feel you are competing with them. Burn them thoroughly in a hot fire (or carry them out of the backcountry).

State fishing laws vary. The following cover the areas described in this book, listed in the order that the tours were taken.

Olympic National Park: No license required in the park, although a special punch card, issued by the Washington Game Department, 600 North Capitol Way, Olympia, Washington 98501, is required to catch steelhead trout.

Yosemite National Park: California state license required. It may be purchased at the Village Store in Yosemite Valley.

Uncompahgre National Forest: Colorado license required for everyone over 15. You may purchase a season license or a 10-day permit for half the price of the license from many sporting-goods stores or inquire of the Colorado Wildlife and Parks Department, 6060 Broadway, Denver, Colorado 80216.

Grand Teton National Park: Wyoming state license required. It may be purchased at Colter Bay or Moose Tackle Shops, at Signal Mountain, and at Leeks Lodge.

Isle Royale National Park: No license required for inland lakes and streams, but a Michigan state license is required for fishing in Lake Superior. Inquire at park headquarters.

Great Smoky Mountains National Park: Tennessee or North Carolina state license required for everyone over 16. Inquire at park headquarters.

White Mountain National Forest: New Hampshire state license required for everyone over 16. Inquire of the New Hampshire Fish and Game Department, Concord, New Hampshire 03301.

A small guide to fishing in the National Parks, Seashores, and Recreation Areas with information on regulations and licenses is available from: Public Documents Distribution Center, 5801 Tabor Avenue, Philadelphia, Pennsylvania 19120. Ask for "Fishing in the National Park System" (S/N 2405–0004; 30¢).

PART TWO

THE TOURS

In the summer of 1975 I flew out to Seattle, rented a car, drove it onto the ferry across Puget Sound, and arrived on the Olympic Peninsula where I met the people with whom I hiked. Afterward, leaving them at an appropriate crossroads, I drove down the Oregon coast into California, then inland to Yosemite. From California I drove across the vast pastel dust of Nevada, into Utah where the earth turned red. Water-carved and wind-whipped, it was chiseled into crumbling monuments of stone that stayed with me as I headed east into Colorado, cutting across the Dolores at Bedrock. Hardly anybody lives in Bedrock. There is hardly anyplace to live. But everybody who passes through stops in at the General Store.

I stopped too—before moving on through old mining towns and past green fields into the cul-de-sac that is Telluride, where I had arranged to meet another hiker. From Telluride I drove north, with a little detour for a few days in Aspen, and on up into Wyoming. Wapiti grazed in the meadows along the road. Cowboys drove lines of horses through the towns en route to the local Friday night

Bedrock Store

rodeo. I joined some hikers in Jackson and we drove out to Teton Village together. I found it hard to leave the Tetons and put it off as long as I could, but finally, with a boat to catch at Grand Portage, began my drive up through Yellowstone, into Montana, North Dakota, and Minnesota.

I can't remember anymore how long the driving took. Enclosed in a car, time has its own sense, measured by day or night and two white lines stretching on and on. Except along Route 101 in Oregon and through Yellowstone until I reached the Lamar Valley, there wasn't much traffic. There wasn't much of anything except space. I flew back to New York from Duluth. There was one plane a day from Duluth to New York.

The tours that follow are not in alphabetical order. They are in the order in which I made them. The Smokies and the White Mountains—familiar territory and therefore not included in the summer of '75—are last because I traveled from west to east.

In all of the tours where it was necessary to backpack—that is, all but Yosemite and the White Mountains—I was with one or two other people. Like most women, I can carry the weight of the necessities for a short backpacking trip, but for longer trips I think it's nice to share the weight, not to mention the sounds in the night. But I like hiking alone, and where there are huts, it is easy enough for me to do it. I mention all of this only because in the chapters on Yosemite and the White Mountains it sounds as if I'm alone. I am. Nevertheless, hiking alone can be dangerous and is not recommended. A minor mishap with someone else there can become a major calamity alone.

There is diversity in the tours. Some, like the Smokies, Isle Royale, or Olympic National Park, are quite easy, barring bad weather. With bad weather, assuming one is properly equipped, they are still easier than the other tours in bad weather. The Yosemite tour is not difficult, but it is at a high altitude, the sun is usually hot, there are some fairly steep ups and downs and, depending on the time of summer you go, some fast water to cross. The Tetons are also high, open, windswept, and early on possibly still snow-covered. However, there is only one trail in the Teton chapter—the Paintbrush Divide—that is really difficult. One can easily ignore that trail, in which case one would have a moderate hike with no particular difficulties, given good weather. The tours in the Uncompahgre National Forest and the White Mountains are not easy. High, steep, rugged terrain awaits you in both places, although there is no comparison of altitudes. The highest point on the White Mountain tour, as well as in the White Mountains, is the 6,288-foot Mount Washington, while in Uncompahgre you *start out* 3,426 feet higher than Mount Washington and cross a snow-covered divide at 13,200 feet.

There is, however, no place where easy trails cannot be found. I have mentioned a few alternate, easy routes in the tour descriptions. If a particular region interests you, go there and explore a little. Instead of following the route described, you might find some extraordinary world I never saw.

The map that accompanies each tour is intended to give you a way to trace the route as you read, but not to substitute for the topographic maps that you should carry.

We are, one might say, off and walking.

1 Olympic National Park, Washington—*From Whiskey Bend to Lake Quinault Lodge*

Rain forests dripping with moss, glittering glaciers sending down cascades of tumbling water, fogbound beaches and cathedral forests of ancient fir—Olympic National Park is prodigious, a lavish world. The Olympic Peninsula lies west across Puget Sound from the rest of Washington. It has the distinction of having the wettest weather in America.*

Most of the park's 1,400 square miles are located just about in the middle of the Olympic Peninsula. It is largely, but not entirely, bordered by Olympic National Forest. There is a 50-mile strip of the park on the Pacific that is one of the most primitive areas in the U.S., a good part of it many miles from any road. The 7,965-foot Mount Olympus, almost smack in the middle of the park, is the highest peak and possesses the three largest glaciers (2 miles or more in length) of the sixty in the park. The trails are, in general, magnificently maintained, even to having drainage

---

* It also has some of the driest. Near the northeast tip of the peninsula, in Sequim, the rainfall averages about 17 inches yearly, or just a bit more than it does in Los Angeles.

ditches dug alongside some which would otherwise become streams after a rain. The signs are clear and handsome, of the same wood as the ranger cabins and the attractive, open-front, Adirondack-type shelters. As in other places where wilderness status is sought for the backcountry, the shelters that fall into disrepair will be removed and not replaced. Most of the camping areas are large and pretty and provide plenty of fairly isolated campsites. Water is everywhere.

A LITTLE NATURAL HISTORY

Because of their northern location, trees, plants, and animals that exist at higher elevations farther south are found at lower heights in the Olympics. The Sonoran zone, sea level up to 3,000 feet in the southern United States, doesn't exist at all in the Olympics. The 3,000-foot to 5,000-foot Transition zone in, for instance, Yosemite, extends from sea level to 1,500 feet in the Olympics. You reach the Arctic-Alpine zone at 5,500 feet here. Most of the tour described, a class cross-Olympic tour from the north side of the park to the south, happens in the Canadian zone—from 1,500 to 3,000 feet. The majority of the trees are Pacific silver fir, western hemlock, and western white pine. At Low Divide this route makes a foray into the Hudsonian zone (2,500 feet to 5,000 feet), which is just below the treeless Arctic-Alpine zone. Here the characteristic trees are Alaska cedar, alpine fir, and mountain hemlock. In the lower regions of the Transition zone are the spectacular Douglas fir, sometimes reaching heights of over 200 feet, the western hemlock, and the western red cedar. In the rain forests you will find Sitka spruce and western hemlock.

Rain forests are produced by heavy annual rainfalls—a minimum of 80 inches to qualify for the name. Primarily tropical, the soil and vegetation of more traditional rain forests differ from those of the park. Up to 175 inches of rain fall annually in the park's rain

Rain forest

forests where year-round temperatures are mild because of the Japan Current flowing by in the Pacific. What the park and tropical rain forests have in common is the growth of unusually tall trees undisturbed by wind, and a dark, lush world. Here everything is green—the evergreens, the moss that grows on tree trunks and drips from limbs, the blanket of moss and fern and wood sorrel that covers the forest floor and the fallen, rotting logs. Seedlings take hold in the richness of those logs, wrap their roots around them, and grow up to be colonnades of trees.

Elk are the most common of the large mammals, but there are numerous black-tailed deer as well. There are also raccoons, skunks, black bears, mountain goats, cougar, bobcats, Olympic marmots (endemic to the Olympics), and mountain beaver (which are not beaver but much smaller rodents about a foot long and weighing two or three pounds. Gray-brown creatures with little eyes, hairless round ears, and a stub of a tail, they burrow into moist slopes). There are also real beaver and otter, muskrat, mink, marten, Douglas squirrels, deer mice, and shrews. In other words, you've got to hang your food up at night.

Anyone hiking on the beach may well see seals in the water or on the rocks, or whales or porpoises. Besides all that, there are about 140 species of birds.

CIVILIZED AMENITIES

Route 101 makes a circle around the Olympic Peninsula, and what other roads there are branch off it. A few paved roads lead into the park, but none goes through it. While every entrance to the park involves being on 101 at some point, the park's north side, the Port Angeles area, is probably the most accessible. Park headquarters and a visitor center are located here 1 mile south of Port Angeles. The trails along the Elwha River, Hurricane Ridge, Deer Park, Lake Crescent, and Soleduck River are all considered within the domain of Port Angeles. Route 101 runs about 10 miles along the southernmost part of the beach section, from Ruby Beach to Queets, but there are no roads at all from Ruby Beach to La Push, all the way north to the end of the park at the Ozette Indian Reservation. La Push and Rialto beaches can be reached by roads from 101 and Ozette by road from Highway 112. The rain forests are nicely arranged so that one, Quinault, falls in the south of the park; another, Queets, in the southwest; and another, Hoh, in the northwest.

Access to the peninsula is either from the south (Route 101) where the peninsula is connected to the mainland or by ferry from the Seattle Ferry Terminal to Winslow, then along Route 305 on the Kitsap Peninsula to the Hood Canal Bridge or, as I traveled, by ferry from Edmonds, 15 miles north of Seattle via Routes 5 and 104. Reservations for cars are not required on the ferries. The Edmonds Ferry leaves approximately once an hour and takes 30 minutes to Kingston where you continue on 104 for 9 miles to the Hood Canal Bridge (toll) and on 104 and 101 for 55 miles to Port Angeles. There is Greyhound service between Seattle and Port Angeles, although once you are there you are dependent on hitch-hiking. (Even with a car you are dependent on hitching unless you make a circular tour or have two cars, since the only bus service on the peninsula is on the northwest side between Port Angeles, Forks, La Push, and Neah Bay. Helpful if you plan to make a beach hike, it is of no use if you follow the route described here, or any of the other routes in the interior of the park.) There is a ferry between Port Angeles and Victoria, B.C., once a day. Bus information: Greyhound, 116 North Albert, Port Angeles, Washington 98362. Ferry information: Washington State Ferries, Seattle Ferry Terminal, Seattle, Washington 98104.

Port Angeles, gateway to Canada and Alaska, is a fair-sized town of about 17,000 people, a waterfront town on the Juan de Fuca Straight. Between the harbor, the lumber industry, and the tourists, it is a reasonably bustling place of no particular character although there is a certain charm in a small corner, where one comes upon an unobtrusive fountain near stairs leading from one level of town to the other. Most of the motels are reasonably priced, and by late afternoon they are fairly well filled. If you have not booked ahead, call along the way as early as possible. A list of accommodations is available from: Port Angeles Chamber of Commerce, 1217 East First Street, Port Angeles, Washington 98362. There are three well-stocked sporting-goods stores where you may purchase freeze-dried foods and backpacking gear, supermarkets, drugstores, and all the other services. The visitor center sells topographic maps, books, and pamphlets about the region.

If you prefer to stay somewhere other than Port Angeles, information about the whole peninsula is available from: Olympic Peninsula Resort and Hotel Association, Seattle Ferry Terminal, Seattle, Washington 98104. For information about lodging in the park, see Appendix C.

SPECIAL REGULATIONS

Parts of Olympic National Park are as overused as anywhere else, but there are, as yet, slightly less stringent regulations than in many parks. As of this writing, only two areas (neither a part of this hike), Flapjack Lakes and Lake Constance, have daily entry quotas (from June 15 through Labor Day). Permits for Flapjack Lakes must be obtained at Staircase Ranger Station, and for Lake Constance at Dosewallips Ranger Station. Telephone reservations may be made for either area by calling Staircase (206) 877-4456 between 8:00 and 5:00. Permits must be picked up in person by 11:00 A.M. on the day of entry. Even where there are no quotas, backcountry permits are required for *all* overnight trips, all year long, and are obtainable at the ranger station in the area where you start your hike. After-hours permits, which you fill out your-self, are in the box outside the ranger station. If you are using pack stock, contact the nearest ranger station for information on regulations. Hiking groups must not consist of more than twelve people and/or eight animals. As in all National Parks, pets, fire-arms, and vehicles are not allowed. While you may still build fires in many areas of the park, there are some where you must use a stove. Ask the ranger. But this *is* a wet area, so carrying a stove is a good idea anyway.

Snow is gone from most of the trails from the beginning or middle of July through October.

BOOKS AND MAPS

Roads and Trails of Olympic National Park, Frederick Leissler, published by the University of Washington Press, Seattle. Paperback, $4.20. The most complete trail guide for the region.

102 Hikes in the Alpine Lakes, South Cascades and Olympics, Ira Spring and Harvey Manning, published by The Mountaineers, Seattle. Paperback, $5.35. The most descriptive trail guide, but includes only selected trails.

Exploring the Olympic Peninsula, Ruth Kirk, published by the University of Washington Press, Seattle. Paperback, $4.95. A complete compendium of all the practical information a tourist needs (trailer parks, boat moorings, laundries, fishing, etc.) as well as a brief social and natural history of the area.

Climber's Guide to the Olympic Mountains, published by Olympic Mountain Rescue. Paperback, $5.95.

Any or all of these books may be ordered from: Recreational Equipment, Inc., 1525 11th Avenue, Seattle, Washington 98130.

The U.S. Geological Survey topographic map "Olympic National Park and Vicinity," scaled at 1:125,000, covers the hike that follows and the entire park.

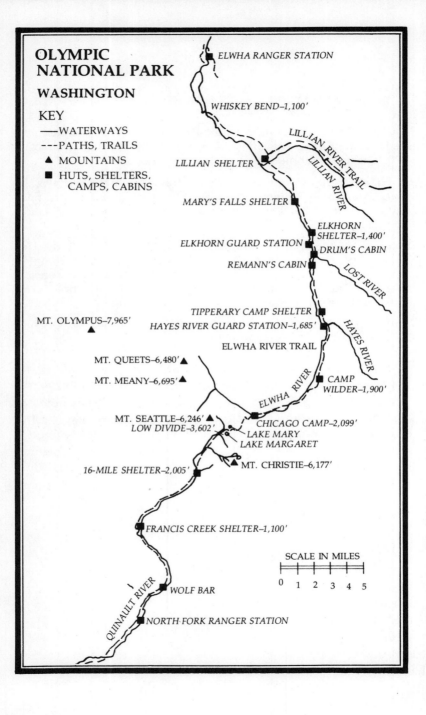

OLYMPIC
NATIONAL PARK

WASHINGTON

KEY
—— WATERWAYS
--- PATHS, TRAILS
▲ MOUNTAINS
■ HUTS, SHELTERS,
  CAMPS, CABINS

ELWHA RANGER STATION

WHISKEY BEND–1,100'

LILLIAN RIVER TRAIL

LILLIAN SHELTER

LILLIAN RIVER

MARY'S FALLS SHELTER

ELKHORN
SHELTER–1,400'
ELKHORN GUARD STATION
DRUM'S CABIN
REMANN'S CABIN

LOST RIVER

MT. OLYMPUS–7,965' ▲

TIPPERARY CAMP SHELTER
HAYES RIVER GUARD STATION–1,685'

ELWHA RIVER TRAIL

HAYES RIVER

MT. QUEETS–6,480' ▲

MT. MEANY–6,695' ▲

CAMP
WILDER–1,900'

ELWHA RIVER

MT. SEATTLE–6,246' ▲
LOW DIVIDE–3,602'

CHICAGO CAMP–2,099'
LAKE MARY
LAKE MARGARET

16-MILE SHELTER–2,005'

▲ MT. CHRISTIE–6,177'

FRANCIS CREEK SHELTER–1,100'

SCALE IN MILES

0 1 2 3 4 5

QUINAULT RIVER
WOLF BAR
NORTH FORK RANGER STATION

Whiskey Bend to Mary's Falls—
8¾ miles, about 4 hours

It was noon, early in July, when the three of us—a couple I had just met and I—picked up our permit at the Elwha Ranger Station, 9 miles west of Port Angeles, then drove 5 miles up the road to the parking area at Whiskey Bend (1,100 ft.) where we packed the food bought in town, lunched on a good deal of it, and finally began our hike on the Elwha River Trail close to 2:00. The trail, level for the first 1.8 miles, winds through majestic Douglas fir, then ascends gently a short ways. At 1½ miles a side trail descends to the Humes Ranch, one of the old homesteads along this route. The trail itself penetrates deeper into the forest, the sunlight spattering through the high trees, focusing here on a single fern, there on a delicate wild flower. At times it rests strong on the side of the mountains. To our right, we glimpse distant glaciers. We cross many streams, most adorned with wooden bridges, although a few small ones are not. There is water everywhere: the turbulent, green, beautiful Elwha (which is reputed to have the best fishing in the park), the smaller rivers that feed into it, the streams bouncing down over rocks and fallen trees to reach the rivers. Four and a half miles from Whiskey Bend is the site of the old Lillian Shelter (1,273 ft.). Shortly before the shelter a path— the Lillian River Trail—heads east from the main path, coming to a dead end 3½ miles up the river.

On the bridge over the Lillian River we encounter a rather large group of girls on horses. Shortly afterward the path begins to climb again, this time up 700 feet in about ½ mile. In the heat of the sun the enormous logs along the beautifully maintained trail provide welcome spots to stop for a cold drink. At the top of this climb we begin a descent of over 700 feet, coming alongside the Elwha for the first time. At 6:00 we stop a few feet this side of Mary's Falls, at a spot where the Elwha is wide, fast, and green, edged on the opposite shore by partially submerged trees. A few feet back from those trees conifers rise abruptly up a rounded, tree-covered mountain. On this side there is a bank a few feet high and a clear space beneath the trees for the tents.

Mary's Falls to Camp Wilder—
12¼ miles, about 6 hours

We leave our campsite, pass the Mary's Falls Shelter (8.8 miles from Whiskey Bend). The shelter directly faces the high, narrow, spectacular Mary's Falls and would be an extraordinary place to wake up in the morning. We climb up a few feet, then walk through forest where moss covers the floors and fallen trees and the huge standing maples, and sunlight streams through the giant Douglas

Morning

*The deer at
Drum's Cabin*

firs that soar infinitely upward. Those that have fallen seem to stretch without end. Awesome. Powerful. It is the first time I have experienced the power of mountains in a forest. Where more light enters, Nootka roses line the path. Nearer the ground, self-heal and bunchberry abound. So do pathfinders whose leaves turn over as we pass through them, their silver undersides then marking the trail. Spiderwebs are everywhere, stretched across the paths from tree to tree, in strands connected somewhere in the middle by the web, wound around the base of trees or strung among the delicate branches of bushes, the light striking both the webs and the single strands so they glitter—ephemeral necklaces. We try to duck under them where we see them so as not to disturb the spiders, but in fact the strands wind themselves around our arms and throats with almost every step.

The trail follows the Elwha, although the river is not always in view, passes the turn-off to the site of the Canyon Camp Shelter (10½ miles from Whiskey Bend), and, 1.7 miles from Mary's Falls, reaches the Elkhorn Guard Station and Shelter (1,400 ft.). Near the Elkhorn Station we come upon a doe and two fawns browsing. The doe pays us no attention, but one of the fawns notices us, stops eating to watch, then realizing he has been left behind, bounds after his mother and sibling. Half a mile farther on we reach the Drum's Cabin. This and another, the Remann's Cabin (1 mile farther on—on the other side of Lost River), are summer cabins left over from pre-park days. I climb the hill to the Drum's Cabin and sit on the porch. After a few minutes a young buck walks up the hill, looks at me with surprise, then comes closer to eat a nearby bush. Finished, he goes back down the hill, investigates my pack, which I have left at the bottom, is joined by a doe, and goes on his way. Another doe lies down like a big dog near where my companions are sitting.

Continuing on, the trail crosses Lost River, passes the Remann's Cabin (1,450 ft.), ascends 235 feet, and arrives, 8 miles past Mary's Falls, at Hayes River Guard Station. Here the junction with the Hayden Pass Trail goes off to the left (east). Just afterward, at Hayes River, one must scramble down the riverbank, then cross wide rapids fairly high above them on a series of three logs. The first two logs lead to the third, which actually crosses the rapids. The log is huge, and a good part of it is covered with wire mesh to keep feet from slipping. While it is wide enough to maintain one's balance, no matter how heavy one's pack, it has no railing and I am relieved when I reach the other side.

The sun is hot and magnificent and a cool breeze has blown all morning. From Hayes River we climb another 215 feet and come, about 4 miles later, still following the river, to Camp Wilder. Here is a large campsite with a shelter. We ignore the shelter, cross a stream on a log, and set up the tents between the river and the stream, near the remains of the old shelter. At 4:00 there is no one else yet here.

Camp Wilder to Low Divide—
7¾ miles, about 4 hours

A few other people arrived at the campsite last night, but they are not yet stirring. The morning is cloudy and still, already humid before 8:00 A.M. We begin our walk, ascending gently through forest that, in the motionless gray day, no longer appeals to me.

The power is gone. We are simply walking through woods like any woods . . . no glittering sun on spiderweb or fern, no breeze. The path soon levels out and we cross the violently churning Godkin Creek where, for the first time today, there is breath and movement. I long to remain on that bridge. A short way on we cross Buckinghorse Creek and then the Elwha, and at each crossing there is the cool relief of the water's rapid movement. At the Elwha, in a confusing clearing, the path is not obvious, and it is not until we have made a brief search that we realize it crosses the stream before us on a log slanting upward to another log which will take us to the opposite side. There we easily pick up the trail, which soon crosses a wooden bridge near the beginning of a swamp. The mosquitos hovering about us all morning now come out in full force. We follow the trail over water and muck, stepping from log to twig to stump to anything to get across, then lose the trail which has, in fact, become a stream. (This is early in the season.) We follow the stream southwest. It soon comes out of the swamp and back into forest. I suddenly feel certain the mosquitos will all be gone when we reach Chicago Camp (2,099 ft.), 5 miles from Wilder and a short way from the swamp. They aren't. There are many pleasant campsites here, although the shelter is falling apart. This is a popular campsite for those climbing Mount Olympus, about 5 miles northwest. (There is no trail all the way to Mount Olympus.) The Elwha River Trail goes about 2 miles in that direction, but stops this side of Mount Queets. Chicago Camp is the point at which our trail leaves the Elwha. We cross the river on a log. I feel sad at leaving it behind, it's been with us so long (25.8 miles, to be exact).

Beyond the crossing the trail begins to climb. This is the steepest climb of the tour. Long and insistent, it switchbacks up about 1,500 feet in approximately 2 miles. Almost immediately after we cross the Elwha the sun comes out, a breeze appears, and the mosquitos vanish. The day suddenly becomes as glorious as the others have been. As we climb we have a beautiful view of Mount Seattle and the waterfall down from Delabar. It takes about an

*Waterfall down
from Delabar*

hour of hiking to reach the top, where we are rewarded by the sight of pretty Lake Mary and, a little farther on, Lake Margaret.

Lake Margaret, still rimmed with large patches of snow in early July, is home to an enormous population of happy and relaxed salamanders—there is nothing here that hunts them. In 1974 a lone seagull did come to the lake for the summer. He had, reportedly, a wonderful time.

There is more snow between Lake Margaret, about ½ mile from the top of our climb, and Low Divide, at 3,602 feet, the highest point on this tour. Because we are so far north, even this low altitude produces a sub-alpine world. We pass through a stand of evergreens where a clearing provides a perfect campsite (with somebody already in it) and head into the vast meadow. All around us are high, jagged peaks of gray rock emerging from great fields of snow. The 6,246-foot Mount Seattle towers in the west, while the 6,177-foot Mount Christie fills our view to the southeast. The rangers are trying to clear the meadow of huge logs, the result of a landslide from the direction of Mount Seattle. We stop at the edge of the meadow, about halfway down, without venturing as far as the shelter on the southern edge.

> *Low Divide to Francis Creek—*
> *9½ miles, about 4½ hours;*
> *Francis Creek to Wolf Bar—*
> *4½ miles, about 2 hours*

The meadow, so hot and sunny yesterday afternoon, is soaked with dew this morning. Everything is wet and the sun is still far from us. We eat and pack in the damp cool. As we cross the meadow we come upon the shelter and a few other tents we hadn't seen, so large is this campground. The ranger overtakes us, asking if we would deliver mail down to North Fork Ranger Station for him. He also tells us that last August—*the* busy time here—3,000 people came through Low Divide. Yet, except for the people camped in the clearing, we had the feeling of being totally alone.

We cross several streams and a few patches of snow. High above us on our right, a waterfall tumbles in a series of grand cascades down from Mount Seattle. Here is the junction, on our right (west), of the Skyline Trail, which comes out 27 miles later on the road a short way below North Fork Ranger Station, or branches off at Three Lakes to follow Tshletsky Creek to the Queets Rain Forest and out to Route 101 east of Queets. (Between Low Divide and Three Lakes the trail remains high up as it follows the divide between the Quinault and Queets watersheds. It is often not passable until

Shelter at Low Divide

August.) We leave the open meadowland behind and once more enter the forest, beginning the steepest part of the now continual descent to Wolf Bar and finally North Fork Ranger Station. Although this descent is less steep than the approach from Chicago Camp, it is about twice the length and far more tiring, and I am glad not to have come up that way. We pass two boys sitting on the trail, farther on a father and daughter, no one else.

We had expected to camp at Francis Creek, 9½ miles from Low Divide, but we are considering going all the way to Wolf Bar, 4½ miles farther on, in order to have a shorter hike out the following day. Four miles from Low Divide we come to 16-Mile Camp (2,005 ft.)—16 miles from the junction of the north and east forks of the Quinault River. The long downhill has already taken its toll on our feet, and we decide to wait until we reach Francis Creek to make a decision about going on or staying. We cross a log bridge over the north fork of the Quinault, the river we will now follow all the way down and come, on the other side, to 12-Mile Shelter—12 miles from the North Fork Ranger Station. We continue near the river for a while until the path begins to climb. We are quickly high above what has become a deep, dark, tumultuous gorge hold-ing a wild, dark river. Glimpsed through trees, raging darkly against rock walls and huge boulders, it has all the fearsomeness of mountain rivers in old lithographs, a dwelling place for fierce and unknown beasts. We cross, shakily, a fast, steep tributary of it, but remain high above. About 8 miles past Low Divide we come to Trapper's Shelter, a small shelter with not much space around it. Tired now, we are eager to reach Francis Creek (1,100 ft.), 1½ miles away, but when we arrive at a shelter marked simply #7, it seems too soon and we continue past it. Just beyond Shelter #7 we lose the path for a moment, but discover that it has once more become a stream, which we follow until it becomes a clear path again. Half a mile beyond Shelter #7 we pass the junction to the right (west) of the Elip Creek Trail, which leads in 4.6 miles to the Skyline Trail. In a silent place the discarded hair of a deer killed by a cougar lies strewn across the trail, the clean bones scattered on the bank of the path. I feel a need to hurry past this territory so specifically claimed.

Farther on we come, to a path branching off to the left and a sign indicating the Half-Way House where a cabin was built to ser-vice the former hunting lodge (now the ranger station) at Low Di-vide. We have come about 13 miles from Low Divide and know well we have covered more than a mile since Trapper's Shelter. Check-ing the map we decide we are, in fact, either very close to Wolf Bar or totally lost. So much for decision making at Francis Creek. Three people approach us. We'll just ask where they came from, we decide. No need to let them know we don't know where we are.

"Where did you come from?" we ask.

"North Fork."

"Oh . . . how far is it?" The nonchalance in our voices is unmistakable.

"You're about three and a half miles from there," they answer, assuming a comforting tone, obviously having mistaken our non-chalance. "You haven't far to go before you're out."

"We're not going out yet," we say, furious with them for their assumption. Suddenly, "We meant to stop at Francis Creek," just bursts out. "But we never found it."

"Oh, you mean Shelter Number Seven. You passed it some time ago. You're only about a mile from Wolf Bar."

Just before Wolf Bar we meet a few more people, out for a stroll. "Have you seen any elk?" they ask. In our weary state we remember only a few frogs, snakes, and slugs and the devoured deer, although of course we had at least seen a number of deer several days earlier. We continue on, looking for elk.

Now the forest becomes rain forest. Wood sorrel covers the floor, moss hangs from the trees. The campsite on the river shore sits in a field of dark, soft grass. Wolf Bar, 2½ miles from the North Fork Ranger Station, to which cars can be driven, is more crowded than any of the other campsites on our way. Tents disgorge countless children who run everywhere through the high grass. Exhausted, we pick a site, then collapse beneath a tree. When we can rouse ourselves we go down to the river and put our feet in the icy water, which numbs and cures them. We build a fire, eat dinner later than usual, and sit around the fire drinking hot chocolate until almost 10:00.

Wolf Bar to North Fork Ranger Station—
2½ miles, 1 hour; North Fork Ranger Station
to Bunch Creek Bridge—4 miles, 2 hours;
Bunch Creek Bridge to Lake Quinault Lodge
—11 miles along the road, a place to hitch

We awake at 8:00, sleepily make breakfast, pack up, and leave. The trail is easy and gentle, if a bit deceiving where it comes down to a broad stream without a bridge but with an obvious trail on the opposite side. Less obvious is the proper trail, which climbs slightly up the embankment on our side, across a stony, dried-up rivercourse marked on its far side by a cairn, then onto a clearly defined path once more which continues through rain forest, over a stream, and around a bend to the left.

By the stream we come upon a woman with three small children. One child sits quietly putting together the bones of the spinal cord of a deer.

"See my puzzle," he says.

A little girl offers us wood sorrel leaves to eat. "They're sweet," she says. They are.

"How big a frog did you see?" the third child asks. I show him with my hands, but it doesn't seem awfully impressive to me so I add that we have also seen some snakes.

"Were you scared?" he asks.

"No, I like snakes," I answer.

"Me too," he says.

We continue on, coming upon an elderly couple who have come to see the rain forest. Then, within minutes, we reach the North Fork Ranger Station, give the mail to the ranger, and begin our hike out. Four miles of dirt road lead to the Bunch Creek Bridge, where several roads combine to provide slightly more traffic. It is still too early (about 9:30) for much traffic to be leaving the campground ¼ mile from the ranger station, but since the rest of the way is by road we would like to hitch. A few cars do pass going in our direction, but the only one not too full to hold us isn't interested in dusty hikers.

We lunch in a meadow full of high grass and a million daisies, bound at the road by tall, dignified foxglove; then continue on, crossing the bridge and beginning to despair of a ride when a man in a large car stops, flips open the trunk for our packs, and invites us in. He has just dropped off his daughter and a friend at the head of the trail through the Enchanted Valley and has great sympathy for backpackers. He drives us directly to the lodge, a rambling old hotel built in 1929 with a vast lawn facing Lake Quinault. The lake belongs to the Quinault Indians, whose land extends from it to the Pacific. There are boats available, and although the lake is not warm, it is swimmable. There is also a pool and sauna and comfortable, pleasant rooms. The lobby is all wicker with the wonderful warmth of a huge old fireplace. Torn between the bar and the

Lake Quinault Lodge

sauna, I decide to have everything—the sauna first, the bar second, and after that a dinner of the superb fresh Lake Quinault salmon . . . and, since we *are* in Washington, Yakima Valley wine.

Lake Quinault Lodge to Whiskey Bend—
about 105 miles

After a 1½-mile hike from the lodge on the South Shore Road (turn right as you leave the lodge) to Route 101, we park our packs by the side of the road and begin to think about the 100-mile hitchhike we have ahead of us—that is, 100 miles from Quinault to Port Angeles. We will actually turn off 101 shortly before Port Angeles to travel the 4 miles to the Elwha Ranger Station, and then 5 miles up the twisting, sometimes steep dirt road to Whiskey Bend to pick up the car. Almost immediately a VW camper stops for us. Inside— the older couple we had met yesterday in the forest. They drive us past white and yellow fields of daisies and high dandelions bound by luxuriant stalks of purple foxglove, sometimes interspersed with a few white foxglove; through what seem royal avenues formed by the deep-green evergreens lining both sides of the road. They drive out of their way (Port Angeles) to take us up to the ranger station, where we begin (reluctantly) the hike up to Whiskey Bend. We are not in the mood for this 5-mile hike under the first threatening sky of the trip. A car approaches with room for one, and I retrieve my car just in time to keep us dry. We, in turn, pick up a few more people on the way down, until there is not an inch of the car not stuffed with people and packs. I deposit everybody at the junction of the road, since I am headed the opposite way from Port Angeles, toward Oregon. I drive back the way we had just come, so that after leaving Lake Quinault Lodge at 8:00 A.M., I am back at the junction of the South Shore Road from the lodge and 101 at 5:30 P.M. I drive into Oregon and rain, and, tired and hungry, come, miraculously, to Seaside where I stop (at the Crab Broiler) for more fresh salmon, then continue on through fog on a winding, empty road to Neskowin and, at midnight, sleep.

/\/\/\

From Whiskey Bend to North Fork was a walk of about 45½ miles. We added a few more miles by continuing on to Lake Quinault Lodge. It is not a difficult route, and while we did it in 4 nights and 5 days, I think it would be nicer to take at least 1 extra day for it, or to add the Skyline Trail and 2 extra days after Low Divide if you are making the tour late enough in the season for the Skyline Trail to be passable.

We were lucky with the weather. Thoroughly prepared for the wettest weather in America, we encountered nothing but sun and clear skies except for the one gray morning and the little bit of rain that fell as we headed back to Whiskey Bend to retrieve the car. I was later told that in summer one can always count on a number of such magnificent days.

2 Yosemite National Park, California—*A circular journey, beginning and ending at Tuolumne Meadows*

It is a hot and dusty July ride through the Sacramento Valley past farms stretching back in both directions. The road is lined with produce stands piled high with mouth-watering displays of oranges and peaches, purple plums and golden apricots, each offering more luscious than the one before. The road climbs up out of this rich farm country into land becoming progressively drier, barer, rockier —empty. Route 120, which I have been following since Manteca, climbs in switchbacks, rapidly gaining altitude until the farm road is lost to sight and the valley has become some distant place. The road passes through Groveland, a lively, one-street, western-looking town where the traffic suddenly becomes thick with pick-up trucks. A few shops—general store, grocery, gas stations—mark the length of the town, after which, with the exception of a few trailers, there is no longer much traffic.

I enter the park at Big Oak Flat, pay my entrance fee, and telephone Tuolumne Meadows to say I will be late to pick up my reservation for the High Sierra Camps. These camps make Yosemite one of those rare places in America where one can remain high up for days at a time without having to camp out. My reservation was to be picked up by 4:00, it is now just about that, and I still have a 45-minute drive from the park entrance on the Tioga Road, the continuation of Route 120 and the only road that passes entirely across the park from west to east.

A LITTLE NATURAL HISTORY

It is a rare world I have entered. The massive granite of these glacier-carved mountains rears up in lopped-off domes, or stands marked in slabs as if they had been built by some great stone-mason. Other peaks, too high to be rubbed and polished by those ancient glaciers, rise in jagged splendor above everything. Water bounds down from the heights to the valley in spectacular falls. It is a rough, rushing, granite-hot world broken by gentle meadows.

Within a day's hike of Tuolumne Meadows there are over 500 different species of plants. Traveling from the Valley to the treeless heights, one passes through all six life zones: Lower Sonoran, Up-

Yosemite rock

per Sonoran, Transition, Canadian, Hudsonian, and Arctic-Alpine. Each one offers its own flowers, or its own season for the same flowers. On the trails described, I passed wild gardens of Douglas phlox, Indian paintbrush, buttercups, and monkey flowers and walked through soft forests of fir and pine and mountain hemlock.

Everywhere, in every direction, Belding ground squirrels scamper over rocks or sit up, straight as little posts, to view the world. Black bears amble out of the trees into the sun, deer browse in deep thickets or lie down at the foot of huge evergreens. Marmots run in and out of their rocky dens and over vast expanses of flat rock. The curious, handsome Steller's jay perches near a tent, and considers.

CIVILIZED AMENITIES

You can reach Yosemite Valley via the express bus that leaves San Francisco Friday afternoons and returns Sunday evenings; or the bus from Merced that meets incoming and outgoing transportation on Amtrak, Greyhound, and Continental Trailways; or the bus from Fresno that connects with both the airport and Greyhound. Amtrak runs from San Francisco and Los Angeles to Merced and Fresno. For more information, write: Yosemite Transportation System, Yosemite National Park, California 95389.

You could base yourself in Yosemite Valley, a very busy place with a variety of accommodations, restaurants, all the necessary services, and bus service (see pp. 39–40) to the high country. But you might find it more convenient—and less hectic—to start out from the Tuolumne Meadows Lodge, a low, sprawling, wooden building surrounded by a multitude of tents. The building houses the dining room and kitchen and serves as a combination lobby and shop where a few small supplies plus some guidebooks (and other books) are for sale and hiking gear is for rent. The tents, where everyone sleeps, are a jumble on the slight hillside opposite the lodge, all of it looking like a cross between the army and summer camp.

The comforts of the Tuolumne Meadows Lodge

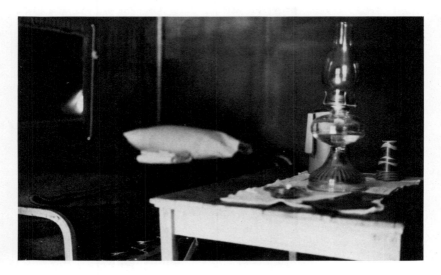

The tents provide comfortable beds for about 120 people. Unlike those in the High Sierra Camps, these are not dormitories, so if you are traveling with someone of the opposite sex you may sleep with him or her. Each tent is furnished with a table, kerosene lamp, potbellied stove, and a bucketful of wood. By evening, smoke issues from the stoves in half the tents; by cold night and in the morning, from all.

Inside, the tents are quite charming, and give one the secure feeling of being in a building. But they are, after all, canvas and in no way bearproof. Bears have often ripped into them in search of food they smelled. Keeping food, any food, even the tiniest bedtime nibble in them, is dangerous. Food should be kept locked in the trunk of your car (or, if you've arrived by bus or by foot, ask someone at the lodge to lock your food in the kitchen overnight). Garbage can be disposed of in bearproof cans in the parking lot, although even these have been known to house an occasional bear.

The people wandering in and out of the tents are a conglomeration of hikers and backpackers using the lodge as a starting or end point. At 8,600 feet, a stay of a night or two in Tuolumne is a good way to acclimate yourself to the altitude of the Sierras. Most people stay a day, then go on. There are, as well, many day hikers vacationing at the lodge and sightseers who come for a night. Rates are, as of this writing, $11.00 plus tax per two-party tent per day. (That is, one or two people pay the same amount.) Meals are not included.

Service in the dining room at Tuolumne is family-style, although everyone cannot be accommodated at once. Write your name on the reservation list when you check in at the desk. Do be aware that the quality of the food is no indication of what awaits you in the high camps. A woman at my table ordered brook trout. Sounded good, I thought. After all, the Sierra lakes are filled with brook trout.

"Is it fresh?" I asked (out of habit) in my turn.

"Oh no," the waitress answered, surprised at the question. "It's frozen. From Japan."

You can, however, buy beer and wine there.

At Tuolumne Meadows there is a well-stocked general store, a snack bar, post office, visitor center (where maps and guidebooks are available), ranger station, and Yosemite Mountaineering, which carries climbing and backpacking equipment for sale and rent, freeze-dried food, and maps and guidebooks. They offer a full program of climbing classes for all levels of climbers (rock and ice) as well as guided (by a ranger-naturalist) weekend backpacking tours. Private instruction and guides are also available. For their brochure, write: Yosemite Mountaineering, Yosemite National Park, California 95389.

The High Sierra Camps (there are five in addition to the lodge at Tuolumne Meadows) are situated about 9 miles apart at altitudes ranging from over 10,000 feet to just under 7,300 feet. Each is a small village of tents plus a main dining tent and kitchen. The kitchen is bearproof (i.e., it is where you store overnight *any* food you're carrying). Each tent, furnished with from four to six comfortable beds, serves as a dormitory. Men and women are sepa-

Tuolumne Meadows Post Office

rated. Linen (including towel and soap) and ample blankets are provided. So, in some of the camps, are potbellied stoves and a bucketful of wood. In all of the camps there are hot showers . . . in a tent, of course. Breakfast (7:30 A.M.) and dinner (6:00 P.M.) are served family-style, and it is good, plentiful, hearty fare.

Reservations are essential. Most people, particularly if they are in a large group (more than one), make them in January and February. Although the summer season extends from early June to mid-September, all of the camps cannot be opened until mid-June or the first of July, because of the snow. It can happen that you reserve beginning with their expected opening date only to be telephoned a short time before with the announcement that late snow has forced a still later opening. Your whole schedule may have to be changed around. As of this writing, rates are $22.50 plus tax per person daily, including breakfast and dinner. For an additional $2.50 they will pack a trail lunch for you. It is an ample lunch and will usually, with the addition of another apple or so, be plenty for two. Many people add a layover day or two at one or more camps in order to fully explore the territory around it. (You need not make the whole circuit. Each camp is a separate entity.) For reservations and information, write: Yosemite Park and Curry Co., Yosemite National Park, California 95389.

After dinner at Tuolumne Meadows I walk out to the nightly campfire a short way above the tents. A ranger-naturalist, encircled by a reasonably rapt group of mostly nonhikers, is talking about the beginnings of National Parks. (Yosemite was one of the first, designated a National Park in 1890, twenty-seven years after 10 square miles of it had been established as the first State Park and eighteen years after Yellowstone was established as the first National Park.) I stay a few minutes, then return to my tent, light the kerosene lamp whose soft glow spreads throughout the tent, throw some wood into the stove, push a little newspaper between the logs, hold a match to it, and within minutes have a warming fire. With the dark the air had become cold. Eager for tomorrow's hike, excited by the prospect of a six-day journey without having to carry backpacking gear, feeling utterly bathed in luxury by the mere thought of it, I fall asleep quickly.

SPECIAL REGULATIONS

Backcountry permits are required if you are *not* staying at the High Sierra Camps. That circuit, after all, covers only a small part of the park's 1,189 square miles. In the Valley you may pick up your permit at the Yosemite Valley Visitor Center; at Tuolumne Meadows there is a backcountry information kiosk (near the ranger station) where permits are issued. You may make reservations for backcountry sites between February 1 and May 31 by writing to: Wilderness Permits, P.O. Box 577, Yosemite National Park, California 95389. (Fifty percent of the capacity of the backcountry is available for reservation; the rest held for first come, first served.) You must provide the following information: (1) dates and points of entry and exit to the backcountry, (2) complete itinerary including route and campsites, (3) number of people and or stock, (4) mode of travel (foot, burro, pack stock, skis). Any change invalidates the permit. If you change your mind once you have a permit, it would be nice if you'd send it back so someone else can use that space. A list of backcountry sites is available from: Pack Superintendent, Box 577, Yosemite National Park, California 95389.

BOOKS AND MAPS

High Sierra Hiking Guide to Tuolumne Meadows, published by Wilderness Press, Berkeley. Paperback, $1.95. Describes all the trails in the area of the High Sierra Circuit as well as the geology, flora, fauna, and history of the area.

High Sierra Hiking Guide Merced Peak, Bob and Margaret Pierce, published by Wilderness Press, Berkeley. Paperback, $1.95. Same sort of guide, but concentrates on the southeastern section of the park and would be useful if you plan to add some layover time at Merced Lake Camp.

Sierra North, Karl Schwenke and Thomas Winnett, published by Wilderness Press, Berkeley. Paperback, $4.95. Includes some of the trails followed on the tent circuit, numerous others that would make good side trips, and many between the high country and Yosemite Valley.

Sierra South, ditto, except it costs $6.95 and, of course, the trails are different. Both are useful if you plan to spend time in the rest of Yosemite. They are clear and informative.

Starr's Guide to the John Muir Trail and the High Sierra Region,
Walter A. Starr, Jr., published by the Sierra Club. Totebook, $3.95.
The classic guide to the John Muir Trail—which wanders through
the Sierras from Yosemite Valley to Mount Whitney, 211.9 miles
away—and the side trails leading into it.

The USGS topo map to use is "Yosemite National Park and Vicinity," scale 1:125,000. Fifteen-minute quadrangles are also available.

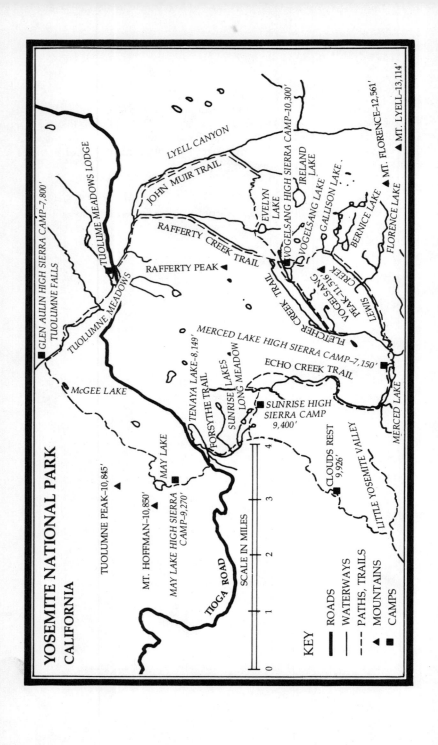

YOSEMITE NATIONAL PARK
CALIFORNIA

GLEN AULIN HIGH SIERRA CAMP–7,800'
TUOLUMNE FALLS
TUOLUMNE MEADOWS LODGE
LYELL CANYON
JOHN MUIR TRAIL
VOGELSANG HIGH SIERRA CAMP–10,300'
IRELAND LAKE
GALLISON LAKE
MT. FLORENCE–12,561'
MT. LYELL–13,114'
EVELYN LAKE
RAFFERTY CREEK TRAIL
VOGELSANG LAKE
BERNICE LAKE
FLORENCE LAKE
TUOLUMNE MEADOWS
RAFFERTY PEAK ▲
VOGELSANG PEAK–11,516'
LEWIS CREEK
FLETCHER CREEK TRAIL
MERCED LAKE HIGH SIERRA CAMP–7,150'
ECHO CREEK TRAIL
McGEE LAKE
TENAYA LAKE–8,149'
SUNRISE LAKES
LONG MEADOW
FORSYTHE TRAIL
SUNRISE HIGH SIERRA CAMP 9,400'
MERCED LAKE
TUOLUMNE PEAK–10,845'
MAY LAKE
CLOUDS REST 9,926'
LITTLE YOSEMITE VALLEY
MT. HOFFMAN–10,850'
MAY LAKE HIGH SIERRA CAMP–9,270'
TIOGA ROAD
SCALE IN MILES
0   1   2   3   4

KEY

▬	ROADS
—	WATERWAYS
- - -	PATHS, TRAILS
▲	MOUNTAINS
■	CAMPS

Tuolumne Meadows to Vogelsang—
6.8 miles, 3½ hours

Day dawns clear and cool. Although I hurry through breakfast in the lodge, there is time enough to discuss the merits of the two routes—Rafferty Creek or Lyell Canyon—to Vogelsang High Sierra Camp. A man who has hiked both trails in each direction a number of times says Rafferty Creek is just as pretty as Lyell Canyon, in addition to being easier and shorter (6.8 miles as opposed to 11.6). It might, he suggests, be the most fun for my first day of hiking at this altitude. Since I might have been persuaded even if he hadn't said it was equally pretty, that problem was easily settled. I pay my bill, put on my knapsack, and set out.

The trail begins behind the tents toward the bottom end of the parking lot. The sign there indicates the JOHN MUIR TRAIL–VOGEL-SANG HIGH SIERRA CAMP, and the path leads south and southeast about 1 mile until it comes to the junction of the Rafferty Creek Trail to the right (south). At this point the John Muir Trail continues on up Lyell Canyon until the Ireland Creek Trail breaks off it to head southwest toward Vogelsang, 4.2 miles past the Rafferty Creek junction.

I no sooner reach the junction than I become lost, somehow noticing neither the junction nor the sign and continue another ¼ mile up the John Muir Trail before I am willing to acknowledge that I must have passed the turn-off. I retrace my steps for about ½ mile, turn again, and come to the junction, this time easily finding the sign set just inside the path, which seems obvious to me now. I wonder at having missed it—but the fact is, there is a sign problem in Yosemite. While all the trails are marked, it is often difficult to *see* the signs, which are made of iron that has rusted; the reddish color blends too well with the trees and earth. Also, the letters are stenciled out, so the words are formed of air. And there are no arrows. The signs are placed on the proper path in such a way that often, by the time you see the sign, you are already *on* the path. Almost everyone I met in the park had some little complaint about

*Mule train en route
to Vogelsang*

them. All the signs are there, so if you come to a place where you feel there *should* be one, look for it. You'll find it somewhere nearby.

The trail continues up along the creek, through woods and over earth and rock, climbing moderately all the way with an occasional level stretch. A few people pass on their way down, and I overtake three girls planning to camp out for a number of days and slowed by their heavy packs. Two mule trains traveling together, carrying supplies up to Vogelsang and on to Merced Lake, pass me. I quickly aim my camera at the first mule driver, a young, handsome cowboy. "Send a copy to Paul Newman," he says, grinning, as he turns square to the camera.

After crossing a creek on stepping-stones, I stop for lunch—a fast lunch, since mosquitos have suddenly converged on me. Cutter's insect repellent keeps them from biting, but they still come to investigate. Afterward I catch up with the mule trains, now stalled in the path because one of the mules, Frances, doesn't like the way her load is balanced. After a good deal of tugging, pushing, and some carefully chosen words—all to no effect—the drivers finally rearrange her load. Frances now deigns to move.

Toward the top of the trail the trees are sparser, and there is more rock until the world simply opens up to rock and sandy earth and sky. Here, where the path crosses flat rock, it is easy to lose it, but impossible to get lost since the "trails" of the mules lead into camp. In the distance in every direction gray, snow-patched masses of mountain rise up against the cloudless sky. The rock masses are marked into rectangles and squares, or chiseled in huge slanting chunks or curves down the mountainsides, rounded and smooth from the succession of glaciers that have carved and ground all this country into its amazing forms. I come upon a marmot who sits unmoving as I stand, unmoving. A little below us three baby marmots poke their heads out of a small hole. A few feet higher I come upon the camp at 10,300 feet, the tents scattered about on the rock, canvas and rock the same, sun-bleached white. Behind the tents the clear, rushing Fletcher Creek sparkles in the sun. It is an extraordinary spot.

I enter the dining tent attached to the stone kitchen, announce myself, am offered lemonade from a pitcher on the counter, and am given a tent facing the stream—so near it that the view from the door window is only of tumbling, rapid water. I immediately incorporate its eternal roar, then spend the rest of the afternoon on the rocks across the stream from the camp, watching, so long as he is in view, a boy climbing Fletcher Mountain. In front of me I have a view to the south of Vogelsang Pass and tomorrow's hike.

The camp's dining room resembles that of a simple alpine hut. The tents all have woodburning stoves. Although we are above tree line and wood is limited, there are logs and kindling in every tent

Vogelsang High Sierra Camp

brought up from Tuolumne Meadows or from lower elevations. In the high, cold night I am grateful for it.

Vogelsang to Merced Lake—
8.3 miles, 4 hours

Breakfast is immense. The same drink offered as lemonade to thirsty arrivers yesterday is, this morning, billed as orange juice. It is followed by French toast, cheese omelet, bacon, rolls, and coffee, hot chocolate, or tea. (A mixture of half-chocolate, half-coffee is the most popular drink.) It is a breakfast that makes me lazy, and I make no rush to leave. I dawdle over coffee, then pay my bill, pick up my food sack (stored overnight in the bearproof kitchen), and make my way through some very bold Belding ground squirrels to the tent.

At 9:00 A.M. I finally leave Vogelsang, crossing Fletcher Creek and heading south toward the 10,700-foot Vogelsang Pass. (The

Fletcher Creek Trail from Vogelsang to Merced Lake leaves Vogelsang heading southwest. It is about ½ mile shorter and lower throughout.) To the east Fletcher Peak is already bathed in sun. The trail
ascends gently, crossing the outlet of Vogelsang Lake and passing
along the west side of the lake. Ahead, in the cloudless morning, is
the pass and, to its right, Vogelsang Peak (11,516 ft.). A few patches
of snow adorn my route to the pass, and in the snow I lose the path
briefly, but see it again quite clearly to the left after a few minutes.
Since it is easily possible to walk anywhere on the bare, open rock
and to see endlessly, straying slightly off the path for a few minutes
hardly seems important. In 1.4 miles I reach the top of the pass,
the highest point of this trip. A wind blows cold in spite of the
sun. Before me spreads a fantastic view—Gallison Lake to the left,
Bernice Lake directly in front, and everywhere beneath the sky gray,
jagged, snow-pocketed mountains. Far to the right, and below, lies
the meadow I will cross and the beginnings of Lewis Creek. I stay a
long time on top. I don't ever want to leave this.

The steep route down (over 800 feet in 1.2 miles) is sheltered

Nearing Vogelsang Pass

*En route from Vogelsang
Pass to Lewis Creek*

from the wind, hot and beautiful. Clumps of wild flowers cling to the sand-colored rock. Two boys with dogs (*illegal on trails, on or off the leash*) make their slow way up, stopping often to rest. On seeing them I realize I've seen no other person all morning. Half an hour later I pass a ranger on horseback. (I found out later that same ranger had already asked them to leave the park with the dogs.) Down, out of rock, I pass an occasional tree, then come to the green meadow threaded with streams running out of Gallison and Bernice, most of which must be forded. (They can be high early in the season, but now, in mid-July, where there are no stepping-stones they are narrow enough in some spots to jump across.) I enter the woods and come to a broad waterfall plunging powerfully down over the rounded, smooth, high, glacier-carved rock . . . a perfect place for my lunch of peanut butter and honey on flatbread, tea, and the fruit I bought at Vogelsang. Afterward, crossing the stream on a log (necessary to retrace one's steps a few feet back from the waterfall), I continue my way down, now following Lewis Creek as it pours over white, wide rock in a world encompassed by the high walls of Lewis Creek Canyon. The creek cuts steeply down while I continue next to it, but now suddenly above it, through woods, then out again to a steep descent that switchbacks over a cobbled path to the Lewis Creek–Fletcher Creek trail junction and Merced Lake Ranger Station. From here the trail turns to the right (southwest) and continues level through a pine forest, then briefly over rock and arrives at Merced Lake Camp (7,150 ft.). In the woods under a tree lies a deer. She watches me as I go by.

The tan Merced tents, arranged in a neat, open-ended rectangle, present a military appearance . . . which turns out to be not at all a false impression. It was once the site of a cavalry outpost. Sitting in front of my tent in the late afternoon, I am visited by both a Steller's jay and a chipmunk. The jay stands around for a while, then flies to a perch nearby and watches. The chipmunk walks up and down in front of me, stands up on his hindquarters, comes nearer, repeats the process several times. When I make no move to give him something to eat, he looks at me in a very odd way and, I am quite certain, stamps his foot.

After a dinner as hearty and delicious as the breakfast (each of the camps serves the same daily menu—although there can be variations in the cooking—so that if you are doing the entire circuit, you will not be served the same dish twice), there is a campfire. All of the camps except Vogelsang, where there is not enough wood available, provide evening campfires. There are usually toasted marshmallows or popcorn or hot cider, singing, a talk by a ranger . . . whatever comes up. This night at Merced is given over to reminiscences of the mule drivers.

Merced Lake to Sunrise—
10 miles, 5 hours

I leave Merced Lake at 8:30 on the level path that leads west out of camp, past the camping area by the lake. Thirty yards from me, next to the lake, a bear lumbers past, headed in the opposite direction, probably making his morning rounds of the campsites. He does not look at me. As I look at him it occurs to me that I am *seeing* a bear walking through the forest. I decide not to photograph him but simply to go on my way without risking drawing attention to myself.

My trail continues over sun-hot rock, smooth, like concrete. Here the route is marked by two lines of stones so that it seems as if one is walking on a sidewalk. The path continues level or slightly downhill to a signpost 2.3 miles from Merced Lake Camp, where the path turns right (north) up Echo Creek Canyon. Here it begins to climb, sometimes in switchbacks, although never very steeply, going in and out of forest, off and on white rock, crossing and recrossing Echo Creek, and coming about 5 miles from Merced Lake Camp to a level, smooth, elegant trail through woods. All along, the way is lined with flaming red-orange Indian paintbrush, purple lupin, owl's clover and the delicate lavender and white Douglas phlox, yellow buttercups and lavender daisies, forget-me-nots and others and others. The woods and rocks are fairly thronged with chipmunks, all on very important missions. I suddenly realize that I am just as excited by each one of them as I had been by the bear—all furred, moving things going about their lives. Several salamanders skitter across the path into the rock.

I come out of the woods to pass, on my left, two cone-shaped mountains. Ahead of me, directly north, is the Cathedral Range with Matthes Crest to the right and Columbia Finger almost straight ahead, west of Matthes Crest. I continue up, past the cones, to a spot where the creek pours gently down over wide rock. I stop for lunch and an hour's idyll in the sun. (An eastern habit; after all, I hardly needed to sit deliberately in the sun after walk-

Long Meadow

ing most of the day in it for so many days.) Beyond my lunch spot the trail climbs again in switchbacks to a pass at about 9,000 feet, then descends to Long Meadow, which stretches out to the north, just below Sunrise Camp at 9,400 feet. The meadow is lush and beautiful, but cut by countless streams, marshy and rife with mosquitos. I had been warned about the mosquitos at Sunrise Camp, but somehow believed they couldn't be as bad as people said. They are worse. Unfortunate, because Sunrise, set on a narrow ledge above the meadow, is a pretty camp. One simply cannot be outside in it. The trail enters the meadow north of the camp, then turns south toward the camp less than a mile away.

When I open the door to the tent, a vast herd of mosquitos enters with me. I take off my pack and spend fifteen minutes killing them (they are about the only things I can bring myself to kill, and I seem to have no trouble doing it), then summon up my nerve to go out again to the shower. By 8:30 at night they disappear, and finally I can go sit on the rocks above my tent to look out on the mountains—the Clark Range to the south and the 12,561-foot Mount Florence to the southeast—and the last glow of the sun over everything. At dusk deer come out to graze on the far end of Long Meadow. A few people stroll on the near end. I stay until the sky is entirely dark and the first stars appear.

Sunrise to May Lake—
8.6 miles, about 4 hours

Sunrise. The sun rises over the dome to the east of camp. The rock I sit on is in sun, the dome behind me in sun, the meadow dark still and covered with a light frost. A Belding ground squirrel runs across the rock in front of me, down to the rock edging the meadow, and disappears. A few birds sing and water pours down out of the rock into the meadow stream. Sun cuts across the southern end of the meadow. Smoke rises from the chimneys of a few tents, but the camp is quiet.

Just below Sunrise Camp there are several extremely confusing signs. (*My* mistake here made this 8.6-mile hike into one of 15.8 miles. I was told—later—that the sign is unclear.) I follow the path that leads southwest from the camp up over rocks, up into a moonscape of a land, silent and dusty. I walk a long way downhill, come alongside Sunrise Creek, into forest, then out along a ridge. Early on when I do not pass the Sunrise Lakes, I know I am on the wrong trail. The trail I meant to take, from Sunrise to the Forsythe Trail, is only about 2½ miles long. After walking 4 miles without reaching that junction, I can no longer ignore my mistake. I sit down to look at the map. The trail I am on leads southwest to Yosemite Valley, about 11 miles from where I sit, or east back to Merced Lake. Another trail heading north would, in under 5 miles, meet up with the Forsythe Trail. The alternative, to return to Sunrise and start over, would make the walk to the Forsythe Trail more than 5 miles. I continue on to the path junction and turn north. Not far from me a bear ambles out of the forest into a ray of sun in a green clearing. The path begins to climb. It seems a long way up the hill, but I suspect it is merely hot. Then, descending, I enter a hot, dry arroyo in which everything—earth, rock, wood—is bleached white, soft, as if powdered with the dust of bones. I cross the arroyo, enter a narrow swamp, and there I lose the trail entirely. I walk straight ahead and climb a brown, boulder-strewn, tree-dotted hill. No sound, no movement, no sign of a trail. I continue up the hill, hoping to see where I am from the top. I am out of water. For the first time in the Sierras, there is no sound of water nearby. I consider going back through the swamp and the dead arroyo, past the bear in the beam of sunlight. Instead I sit down on a rock, facing the way I had come. Suddenly, on my left,

View along the wrong way

not more than a few feet from me, is a trail junction: the meeting of the Forsythe and Sunrise Lake trails. I am not lost anymore.

When *you* leave Sunrise Camp, follow the path that heads directly across the end of the meadow, not the path on your right as you face the meadow; unless, of course, you'd like to try your luck with bears, arroyo, swamp, etc. The proper path descends from the camp's ledge and heads west, then northwest to Sunrise Lakes, climbing slightly at first, then descending gently for 2½ miles to the junction of the Forsythe Trail with the trail leading south to Clouds Rest (and ultimately to Yosemite Valley). From here, at 9,180 feet, the way descends steeply down Tenaya Canyon over a stony path in a series of switchbacks, to arrive 2½ miles later at Tenaya Lake (8,149 ft.).

As I descend I look out over mountainsides that are simply slabs of tree-dotted granite, that seem laid down over the mountain. I am used to jagged peaks—nowhere have I seen such mountains as these. (Tenaya Canyon has the largest area of exposed granite in the park.) To the west there is a view of Mount Hoffmann (10,850 ft.), which is where I am headed (May Lake sits at its foot), and, north of Mount Hoffmann, to the 10,845-foot Tuolumne Peak. I descend quickly. There are many people on their way up this popular path, the first time since I left Tuolumne Meadows that I have seen more than two or three people on the trail.

Approaching the lake the trail levels out and leads into the campground. A seagull swims at the edge of the lake. I cross the stream (Tenaya Creek) that flows from the lake's south end (on my right as I descend from the Forsythe Trail) on a long series of stepping-stones, then follow a path at the edge of a meadow that leads to the Tioga Road. This is the only time on this hike that I even see a road, much less have to walk on one. I find it, not oddly, jarring. There are not many cars on it and it is very hot. I turn left and walk up the road about ½ mile, finding, on the right-hand side of the road, two wooden posts with orange-painted rectangles cut into them, marking the old, unpaved, abandoned Tioga Road.

(There is no sign.) The path leads up this road for 2.4 miles until it reaches Snow Flat, where there is a campground accessible by car (from a road off the Tioga Road, farther to the west), then continues gradually up, through woods and over rock to May Lake (9,270 ft.) 1.2 miles later.

Although it is the 19th of July, patches of snow still cling to the ground around the tents and dining hall of May Lake Camp. The lake glitters in the late afternoon sun. Behind it Mount Hoffmann rises up, abrupt, singular, cutting off all the world to the west. (A hike to its 10,850-foot summit makes a nice afternoon's side trip. It should take about 2½ hours up, 1 hour back down, on a trail marked with cairns.)

At sunset I climb up onto the rocks that wall in the camp on the east side to see beyond them to the eastern mountains and the colors of sunset they reflect. For the first time on this trip the sky is streaked with clouds, so there will be colors in a sunset at last. I had waited nightly for this. I look out east toward the Cathedral Range and watch it glow with rose that seems to radiate out of the mountains. The color darkens, disappears. The mountains take on the luminescence of the almost-full moon until night comes on too far and only their dark shapes are left, and the moon and stars are left.

May Lake to Glen Aulin—
8.2 miles, under 4 hours

Leaving May Lake at the north end of the lake, the trail crosses bare white rock marked with rows of stones, then descends in switchbacks over stone and sand until, leaving the hot, beautiful rock entirely, it enters woods, coming soon to the junction of the trail to Ten Lakes. A party coming up on mules has stopped to rest at the junction. Some backpackers on their way up from Glen Aulin have also stopped. I continue on through forest, descending still, but more gently now, coming half a mile farther on to the junction of the Murphy Creek Trail to Tenaya Lake. I find this path through

McGee Lake

woods no longer especially interesting. The trees are not unusual;
there is barely a view of rock; the wild flowers are neither lush nor
rare. A small, hurt bird lies in the path. There is nothing I can do
for it but leave it to be killed by some other animal. I find a small,
dark snake resting on a rock in Cathedral Creek. Finally I come to
McGee Lake—beautiful, still, surrounded by pines. Mount Con-
ness rises up at its northern end. Here is a lovely spot for a swim.
From the lake it is only about 1 mile to Glen Aulin, at 7,800 feet.

Near the camp the trail climbs a bit only to descend immediately, then crosses the Tuolumne River twice over bridges. On the
bridges I can feel the spray of the thunderous Tuolumne Falls,
which give this camp its special character. Around the camp the
earth is sand; by the river, the sand turns very white and hot. The
river, cold, deep, and swift until early July, becomes shallower
and perfectly safe for swimming by mid-July.

On the ridge of rocks that shelters the camp in the west, I watch the sun set while simultaneously the full moon rises in the east. One glows with fire, the other with memory.

Glen Aulin to Tuolumne Meadows—
6.8 miles, about 3 hours

After eating twice as much breakfast as usual (it was my last in the camps and I hated to let go of that kind of succor), I am on my way at 9:00 A.M. to ascend to Tuolumne Meadows. I cross the two bridges, then head left (southeast), begin to climb gently, and soon come out of the trees to open rock, cross the river again, and arrive at a vast, open expanse of sloping, flat rock. A marmot sits on a small boulder, then scurries around to the back of it when I try to photograph him, and proceeds to examine and scratch his entire body. I hear another one behind me and turn to see him sitting full in the hot sun on the open rock. He poses for his picture. Continuing on, I come again to woods where a doe breakfasts on leaves. She watches me, retreats a few steps deeper into the forest, then goes on eating.

Marmot

Now many people begin to pass me on their way to Glen Aulin from Tuolumne Meadows, a very easy hike. Here are hikers and backpackers and tourists out for a stroll, an assortment I have not seen on any other trail. A ranger rides by and asks about my back-country permit. I say I was staying at the camps (and therefore do not require one). A ranger had passed—and asked—every day except the day I was lost. A mule train passes. A group of tourists on horses approaches, led by a cowboy whom I photograph without recognizing. "You send that one to Paul Newman, too," he says. The tour has come full circle.

I reach the meadow above Soda Springs at noon, cross it in the hot sun, and come to the Tioga Road, which I cross to continue to Tuolumne Meadows Lodge on a dirt path. If I had walked on the road, I would have come to the store, snack bar, and post office.

Out of Yosemite on the Tioga Road, heading east now, I drive over the Tioga Pass into Inyo National Forest to Lee Vining and Mono Basin and on into the empty desert.

/\/\/\\

In doing this route again I might spend more than one night at some of the camps, particularly Merced, so that I could make some side trips from there.

I met many older people on this hike—experienced hikers who enjoyed spending days at a time in the backcountry but were not interested in backpacking. I welcomed their diversity, a diversity possible, and in evidence, wherever there are huts of some sort. Unfortunately, the whole future of the camps in the park is up in the air, probably until 1977, when a master plan for the future of Yosemite, currently being developed by the National Park Service with the help of public opinion, will be ready for approval. That plan might involve the elimination of the camps entirely, or the use of them in a more limited way, with the camps providing food and shelter and the user bringing in his own bedding and towel. But the decision could also be in favor of maintaining them as they are or even adding new camps. While most decisions concerning the future of the park may have been made by the time you read this book, it may still be of use to send any thoughts about maintaining the camps to your congressman, the National Park Service (see address in Appendix B), or the Yosemite Planning Team, c/o Golden Gate National Recreation Area, Fort Mason, San Francisco, California 94123.

3   Uncompahgre National Forest, Colorado—*A round trip through the Wilson Mountains, beginning and ending near Telluride*

At 6:00 A.M. Telluride was silent, damp, and gray. A piece of sky tried, vainly, to dispel the clouds that finally took it over. The streets were empty, save for a few night-wet dogs who looked at me with suspicion. One barked, all slunk away. They, or I, had done something wrong. On the main street crows walked up and down in front of the post office. A girl in jogging clothes ran out of a side street, across the main street, and up toward the hill behind the Manitou Inn. I walked down muddy back alleys littered with trucks and carts. A black cat watched, disappeared in a doorway, followed by a gray cat I hadn't seen. At the end of the road, at the feet of the wild, 14,000-foot San Juan Mountains, the town ends.

Colorado, one hundred years younger than America, is filled with towns like Telluride, improbably lodged high in narrow valleys, their whimsical Victorian façades left over from a raw time when men built dreams of silver and gold. Ladies in long, flowered dresses go about the day's errands. Bearded men, small children, and large dogs spill out of the shops and cafés. Pick-up trucks and

Colorado street scene

jeeps drive in and out of town. It is a world that exists in two centuries. It is the most relaxed place I've ever been.

Many of the old mining towns, bustling in the late nineteenth century, then left almost to die, have been physically restored and turned into ski towns. They are filled with good restaurants and shops, a variety of lodging, and no end of atmosphere.

Here, more than anywhere else in America, is the possibility of hiking from town to town over the mountains. Among the most popular of all Colorado hikes are the routes from Aspen to Crested Butte. The trail over the 11,800-foot East Maroon Pass is about 20 miles long; those over the 12,750-foot Pearl Pass and the 11,928-foot Taylor Pass are both about 28 miles long. Once the Colorado Trail is finished, it will even be possible to hike from Denver to Durango. The road distance between the two places is about 340 miles, but the trail will stretch for about 550 miles, passing through six National Forests and including a multitude of loops so that one can enter and leave it at numerous points in between. A good part of the trail already exists. For information, contact: U.S. Forest Service, Federal Center, Building 85, Denver, Colorado 80225.

In addition to a great amount of National Forest land, Colorado possesses two National Parks. The 405 square miles of Rocky Mountain National Park in the north straddles the Continental Divide, while the 120 square miles of Mesa Verde National Park in the southwest—the only National Park established to protect something man-made—offers a radically different landscape in the hot canyon lands out of which the protected, ancient cliff dwellings have been carved. Like most other places, Colorado has its share of overused wilderness. In areas like Maroon Bells in White River National Forest near Aspen (through which the shorter Aspen–Crested Butte Trail passes), the Forest Service would like to see fewer hikers.

A LITTLE NATURAL HISTORY

The hike that follows, which begins and ends a few miles from Telluride, was selected partly because it wanders through some of the least-crowded backcountry in the state. Most of the route described lies within Uncompahgre National Forest, although the last part of it, from the west side of the Rock of Ages Saddle to Lizard Head Pass, goes through the adjoining San Juan National Forest. The whole area is made up of rugged mountains reaching over 14,000 feet, fast streams and deep canyons, small lakes, wondrous meadows, and endless ruins of old mines. It is supposed to abound in wildlife—deer, elk, bears, bighorn sheep, wild turkeys, ptarmigan, grouse, and trout—but I have seen only an elk, a family of ptarmigan, and an assortment of small animals.

Although there are rumors of grizzlies in the San Juan Mountains, I was told that, in fact, there are no grizzly bears in the Mount Wilson area (the focal point of the hike that follows) and that even people who live in the area and hike there all the time almost never see sheep. Animals in National Forests, where they are hunted, are of course shier than those in National Parks, where they are not.

The wild flowers are not in the least shy. In late July whole hillsides are fairly bursting with columbine, clumps of tall chiming bells, and harebells. Indian paintbrush, phlox, and buttercups are everywhere. Meadows full of the monumental green gentian are edged by stands of quaking aspen and forests of pine, Douglas fir, and Engelmann spruce. The evergreens, straight and tall in the Transition and Canadian life zones (8,000 to 10,500 feet), are windblown, and dwarfed as they extend higher up through the Hudsonian zone to timberline.

CIVILIZED AMENITIES

Butch Cassidy robbed his first bank in Telluride. In his day it was a wide-open town that supported two banks, four dance halls, and twenty-six each of saloons and bordellos. William Jennings Bryan made his famous "Cross of Gold" speech in front of the Sheridan Hotel. The hotel hasn't changed much. The whole town, in fact, has been designated a National Historic Landmark by the U.S. Department of the Interior.

Telluride can be reached only by car (or by foot). United and Frontier airlines fly into Grand Junction, 127 miles away, and Frontier flies into Montrose, 66 miles from town. Car rentals are available at both airports. Limousine service to and from Grand Junction and Montrose is available from: Telluride Transfer, 13 West Pacific Street, Telluride, Colorado 81435; (303) 728-3961 days, or 728-3759 nights.

There is a variety of lodging, ranging from the Home Dormitory on East Colorado Street next door to the Upper Crust Bake Shop to the luxury of condominiums (rented like hotel rooms) on the west end of town. A list of accommodations is available from: Telluride Chamber of Commerce, Box 653, Telluride, Colorado 81435; or telephone Central Reservations (303) 728-4316. The Home Dormitory may not be on their list, but as of this writing it costs $3.00 per night with your own sleeping bag, or $5.00 per couple with sleeping bags. Showers for 50¢ are open to the public.

As for restaurants, ideally one should stay long enough to try them all. My favorite was the Senate, but I'm not sure it wasn't just because I like going through swinging doors. The Senate was one of the twenty-six saloons, and there is still a bullet hole in the floor from a shot fired at the local sheriff. He must have been a very short sheriff.

Among the many shops are several selling hiking and mountaineering gear, and of these, the one to go to for the largest stock —gear, food, and maps—is Olympic Sports, next door to the Floradora Saloon. (Then go to the Floradora Saloon.) Maps and the best selection of books about the area are available at the Wagner Art Gallery, 120 North Fir, just north of the drugstore. The Wagners are experienced hikers and know the region well. Mr. Wagner's paintings, on view at the gallery, take these mountains for their subject.

SPECIAL REGULATIONS

No permits are required for this tour. For further information about Uncompahgre National Forest, write: Forest Supervisor, 11th and Main Street, Delta, Colorado 81416. The nearest ranger station to Telluride is in Norwood, about 30 miles northwest of town on Highway 145.

The season here is about mid-July to mid-September. Ordinarily one can count on a brief afternoon thundershower in the

Rockies, but this year was unusually wet. There was also late snow all over the West. Anyone following my route over the Rock of Ages Saddle between Gladstone Peak and Wilson Peak may find a totally different mountain from the one I climbed. There is often far less snow on it than I encountered, and it could well be sunny. The weather conditions had a great influence on the number of miles we covered each day. They weren't many. This is difficult, steep, high terrain and would have been slow (for me) even in the best of weather. Where the terrain was not so difficult, we were the first hikers over it in thirty years, which, of course, presented most of the difficulties inherent in bushwhacking. By publication date that particular unused trail should be well used, marked, and easy to follow.

BOOKS AND MAPS

There are no guidebooks for the area, but William Grout in his book *Colorado Adventures,* published by the Golden Bell Press, 2403 Champa Street, Denver, Colorado 80205 (paperback, $3.50), describes a three-day backpacking trip in the Wilson Mountains from Bear Creek Road over the Rock of Ages Saddle, Navajo Lake, Woods Lake to Silver Pick Basin and back to Bear Creek Road. His book includes hikes, drives, jeep trips (very popular here— inquire at Telluride Transfer), and backpacking trips. Trails are not described in detail, but the book would be useful to anyone planning a trip to Colorado who is not entirely sure of what to do there. In all, he describes forty short trips.

A few other books, available at the Wagner Art Gallery:

A Quick History of Telluride, Rose Weber, published by Little London Press. Paperback, $1.95.

Mountain Wild Flowers of Colorado and Adjacent Areas, Ruth Ashton Nelson and Rhoda N. Roberts, published by the Denver Museum of Natural History. Paperback, $1.50.

Guide to the Colorado Mountains, Robert Ormes, published by Colorado Mountain Club. $7.95. Available from the club, 2530 West Alameda Avenue, Denver, Colorado 80219; this is of no specific use for a hiker following this route.

The New Aspen Area Trail Guide, Michael O'Shea. Paperback, $1.95. Available from him, Box 15042, Aspen, Colorado 81611. This has nothing to do with Telluride; I mention it only because I have mentioned hikes that it covers.

You need two USGS topo maps for this tour: 7.5-minute series "Dolores Peak" quadrangle and 7.5-minute series "Mount Wilson" quadrangle.

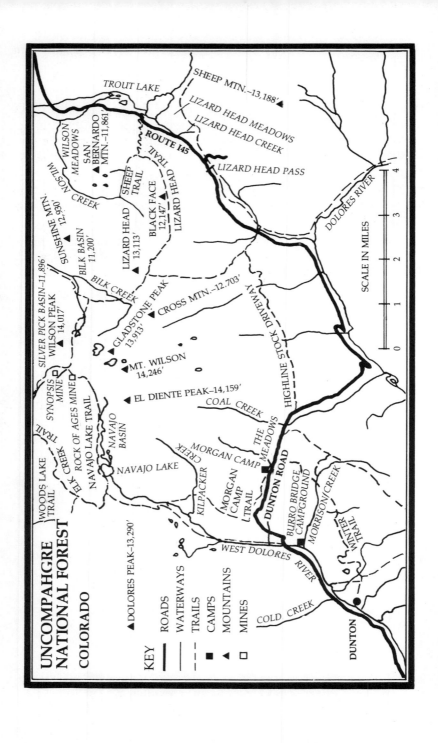

Trout Lake to Lizard Head Trail to the
Sheep Trail—under 1 mile, about 1 hour

Trout Lake (9,714 ft.) is about 11 miles from Telluride on Highway 145. You may park your car there, then turn left and hike
up the road about ¼ mile, cross the road, and come to a sign indicating the beginning of the Lizard Head Trail. The trail begins to
climb, immediately and steeply, up a meadow, through a grove of
aspens and fir.

Two of us begin to hike in the late afternoon, trudge upward,
past great clumps of dwarf columbine, under a threatening sky.
Thunder rumbles in the distance. We pass the ruin of an old log
cabin. A short way beyond the cabin, after about an hour's hike
from Trout Lake, we come to a meadow at 10,800 feet, encircled by
evergreens. Here the sheep trail to Wilson Meadows branches off
the Lizard Head Trail. Wilson Meadows provides a lovely campsite
if you don't mind going ½ mile out of your way. The trail junction
is marked by a post with the initials *LH* and an arrow carved into
it, indicating the Lizard Head Trail to the left (southwest), while
the sheep trail continues straight ahead.

The sky has darkened now and the thunder comes nearer. Because of our late start from Trout Lake, we decide to camp here.
There is a fire ring at the edge of the forest on the west side of the
meadow, below the sign. Sitting on a luxurious log next to the tent,
I look out over Trout Lake and behind it to mountains striped
orange, red, green, yellow, and gray, the layers of rock curving
around a snow-filled bowl. Beneath everything is evergreen forest.
There is no water at this campsite, but we brought up plenty from
Telluride. The storm holds off until we have eaten and are in the
tent, then comes without fury. In the morning a crashing and
scraping sound in the woods wakes me, and I look out in time to see
an elk rubbing his antlers against a tree.

From the Sheep Trail to Bilk Creek—
about 2½ miles, about 2½ hours. (An
additional 3 hours was spent wandering in
search of a path, and waiting out a hailstorm.)

The path leaves the post and ascends steeply through spruce and fir for about 45 minutes until it comes out onto open meadow. From the edge of the meadow (a side track from the route, which continues to the right), there is a view of Trout Lake, Lizard Head Meadows and, beyond them, of Sheep Mountain (13,188 ft.) and the same striped mountains I had seen from camp. There is no definite path at first across the meadow, but the route heads southwest (to the right) through more spruce. A defined path appears and disappears beneath your feet as you come to open meadow where you may walk anywhere. In the distance to the left, wooden posts mark the direction you should take, magnificently, openly following the ridge as it climbs up to 12,147-foot Black Face. The wind here is powerful, and in spite of the hot sun I stop to put on a sweater. Lizard Head, the core of an ancient volcano that has fallen away, emerges adamantly into view. It does, indeed, look like a lizard's head.

From Black Face the trail descends, nicely marked now by little pickets, until it enters a beautiful but irrational thicket. This whole area of low-lying shrub is a maze of what seem to be paths, all of which lead directly into an impenetrable clump of green. The route heads west, down through the thicket on any line you choose, and ultimately rounds Lizard Head to the north of the trail and northwest of the thicket. Hoping to come out of the thicket not too far off the path, we head for the woods below the thicket (having finally decided to abandon trying to make sense of the little paths within the thicket) and do, fairly easily, pick up the trail. At the bottom of the woods there is a stream (not shown on the topo map). Follow the stream up, keeping Lizard Head on your right.

The way climbs easily, and at its highest point wooden posts again appear to mark the way. The trail now remains well defined

Lizard Head

as it edges Lizard Head, offering remarkable views of it from a number of directions. Incredible fields of wild flowers: buttercups and columbine, bell flowers and clover, yellows, blues, and reds like garnets stand out brilliant against the gray stone and scree and the gray—deepening, threatening gray—of a storm-portending sky. Suddenly we come upon a landscape wholly new and foreign. A wide stream bisects the valley spread below us, the valley all grass and rocks until it descends to a region of evergreens. Surrounding every-thing—the valley, the trees, us, the flowers we have come through—are vast mountain walls of red, copper, green, and gray. The gray sky emphasizes the colors.

It is so empty and silent and I am so transported in it that I suddenly find myself looking about for a band of Chagba (brigands who dwell in the mountains of Tibet), whose arrival I feel is inevitable. (I would probably seem so poor to them that they would more likely give me something than take something away, honorable bandits that they are.)

Closing in the far (northwestern) end of the valley is 14,017-foot Wilson Peak. A steep switchback winds part way up its side. From here it looks very high and steep. It is tomorrow's route.

We descend to the stream and refill the water bottles. The thunder that has accompanied us, but distantly, for the past hour is nearer. The sky is completely gray now and the storm will break soon. The stream is fast, deep, and cold, and we find no place along it narrow enough to jump, although we walk it in both directions, looking. There is nothing for it but to walk through it, across it. No sooner are we on the other side than the rain starts. We walk quickly away from the stream, lay our packs down against the side of the path under a bush, and grabbing our raingear, settle ourselves under another bush some distance from the packs just as the full force of the storm breaks over us: lightning, thunder, hail. The bush gives us some protection from the hail, and with the lightning past and the hail turned to rain, we once again pick up our packs and go on our way.

The path climbs very slightly now, and in a short way we come to another path branching off to the left. While there is no sign, we decide this is the path that leads up to the Rock of Ages Saddle. (This is not the switchback mentioned earlier.) For now we continue straight on, eager to descend to tree level in Bilk Basin to set up camp. We cross a creek that tumbles down over the path and with the rain increasing in force, arrive at Bilk Basin. We lean our packs against a log and take shelter under a stand of evergreens, believing the storm *must* soon pass by. It doesn't, and the force of it and the wind penetrate our ponchos. We become cold and, in a fairly desperate state, hurriedly put up the tent (which afterward sagged a good deal, but remained standing), throwing the rainfly on top as soon as the tent was out of its sack. Then, chucking the sleeping bags and dry gear inside, we scoot in after. Five-thirty. Shivering, we put on dry clothes and wiggle into the bags. We have taken a bag of chocolate, raisins, and nuts in with us. Even though we had been told there were no bears here, it was only our desperate need for calories that led us to this sin of all sins. It is more than an hour before we feel warm. Meanwhile the storm continues with its full force, and the chocolate, raisins, and nuts turn into dinner. Warm, we sleep a few hours, then wake to discover we have pitched the tent on rocks (the only flat place in our rush) and cannot sleep the rest of the night. The rain seems to slacken, but the wind howls and beats against the tent.

From Bilk Basin to Navajo Lake—
about 2 miles, about 4 hours. (An additional
hour was spent wandering about an
impassable trail.)

We awake to miraculous sunshine, eat an enormous breakfast, and head back toward the fork we had passed yesterday. Turning to our right at the fork we begin immediately to climb. In a high meadow, at a snow-covered stream, we run out of path. The snow is arched high in places across the stream, which breaks out to run rapidly over jagged rocks a number of feet below the snow. Maybe the snow will hold if we cross it, but it seems risky. Where the stream is not covered it speeds downhill, encased in a steep little canyon with vertical, slippery walls. Checking the map we decide the switchback trail we have been looking at since yesterday will also take us to the saddle. We make our way down along the stream edge to rejoin the path past Bilk Basin. Stones bridge the stream where it crosses the path. (I mention this "wrong way" because, in fact, we *could* have reached the start of the route up to the saddle by it. It is a way that is used. We were told that the snow "probably" would have held, but I would try it only if there were no snow.)

We reach the bottom of the switchback, having spent over an hour on our wrong route, and begin the long trek upward over occasional patches of old snow. Our morning sun has disappeared, the sky is gray once more, and we have hardly begun to climb when the first drops of rain fall. A frightened mother ptarmigan tries to look like a rock in the path, her wings spread in a futile attempt to protect her fledglings, two of whom run up the mountain and one down. Waddling and flapping, she cannot get them under her wings. I pass as quickly and discreetly as I can. It is slow going as we climb up from the 11,200 feet of Bilk Basin to 12,063 feet in less than ½ mile, where we come to a little lake and the ruin of a miner's cabin. Here, at last, we have reached the base of our climb up to the Rock of Ages Saddle. To the right is Wilson Peak, to the left the 13,913-foot Gladstone Peak. Curving in front of us, above us, is a high, steep, snow-covered bowl, a few rocky outcroppings interrupting the empty whiteness, the rocky top of the 13,200-foot saddle crowning it all. It is just over ½ mile from the lake to the top. The rain persists. It is a cold, bleak landscape that faces us. We add gloves to our raingear, then begin our first traverse along a long snow slope on the north side of the bowl.

Suddenly we are aware of two people standing on one of the rock outcroppings high above us, on the opposite side of the bowl. We are glad to know we are not alone in this forbidding world. (How different it would be on a sunny day!) But since they are on the opposite side we check our map. Should *we* be over there? We decide our route is correct and continue, coming, at the end of the traverse, to a steep slope. Each step must be kicked into the snow. Occasionally a foot slips, slides, recovers.

We go up and up, slowly up, the weight of the pack too much, the altitude still too new, the snow and gray damp endless. But I, at least, feel more secure facing the slope and climbing up than I did traversing. There, in a traverse, where I can see the icy pond beneath me and the long slide down to it, I feel far more the weight of the pack as an unbalancing, inevitable pull downward, and there I am terrified of slipping. If I slip facing upward, I need only dig my hands and toes into the snow to stop myself. Slowly I continue up, digging in one foot, then the next. A ladybug walks across the snow just above my step. It seems to me an enormous

*The walk up to
Rock of Ages Saddle*

world for her. At the top of this slope we reach a wet, cold island of
rock, where we stop for a fast lunch, then cross the rock and begin
another traverse to still another island, this one capped with a
miner's cabin. Still the rain continues. The two people we saw
earlier (and had since forgotten) now appear on top of the saddle.
We call to them, "Can you see the trail down?"

"Yes," they answer. "Very much like the one up."

"As much snow?" we ask.

"Lots of snow. We can see Navajo Lake. It looks far."

I somehow thought they would describe the way down as a
gentle, sun-filled path lined with columbine. The cabin, exposed as
it is, seems to offer meager shelter, although going on through the
snow and endless rain offers even less comfort. But we can't turn

back. I'll be damned if *I'm* going down what we just came up. In spite of its bleakness, I wonder if it might not be possible to spend the rest of my life in the cabin. While I consider that, I begin to feel cold. The rest of the way starts to seem possible; a traverse to a rock outcropping that will take us to about the center of the bowl, a short climb up a snow ridge, a rock scramble, a little more snow, then more rock to scramble over to the top. We start out, the traverse again difficult for me, but the rock comfortable and fun. On the traverse, inexplicably, the sun comes out. Now anything is possible.

We reach the top to find the couple still there. They have been up there a rather long time. They like it there. We sit on top for a while, looking down over Navajo Lake more than 1,000 feet below, while directly beneath us is steep rock and more snow. To our right is the old Rock of Ages Mine and a part of the trail down. A large group of hikers winds its way slowly up the right (west) side

View of Navajo Lake from Rock of Ages Saddle

of the snow bowl before us. The couple, who are in their twenties, came from Arizona, have hardly ever hiked, and are finding the whole experience—rain, cold, and snow included—a lark. They had camped the night before near the miner's cabin at the lake at the base of the climb. When they finally descend and are free of the rocks, we watch them sit down on their parkas and slide down the snow slope.

We start down ourselves. None of us noticed the proper route, the way to our right. (It crosses the entire jagged rocky part of the saddle before descending, still on the saddle ridge, to a lower area of scree and then crosses the face of the wall, down to the Rock of Ages Mine.) We all go straight down, scrambling over massive, jagged boulders, landing finally in the snowfield. This one, mercifully, is not too steep to be fun. We cross another island of talus, come to another snowfield. Suddenly, with no warning, lightning and hail fling themselves upon us. Hurriedly leaving our packs against one rock, we find shelter against another rock in a small outcropping of meadow some feet away. We hold an extra poncho over our heads for some additional shelter from the large hailstones beating down on us. They gather quickly in every fold of my poncho, as they do on the meadow. Within minutes the heads of buttercups poke through a field of white. Ahead of us the tracks in the snow of the other two people are quickly obliterated. Behind us, in the direction we had come, the group we had watched from the saddle continue their climb, reaching the saddle ridge (on the proper trail, which is easier to see from this side of the saddle than from the top). They walk along the ridge, then disappear over the saddle. We wait until both hail and lightning end, pick up our packs, and continue, wearily, on our way across more snow to another ruin of a miner's cabin and the end of the snow. Here we find a wooden post marking the trail and a well-defined trail across rocky and soggy meadow to a path of scree. The rain stops. Two marmots run down from the mountain on our right to somewhere below us. We continue down, coming, at last, to Navajo Lake. The couple above us is already setting up camp. We remain on the east side of the lake and set up our tent in a site not very far from the river. We eat dinner in sunlight.

From Navajo Lake to the Winter Trail—
about 6½ miles, about 4 hours

We leave Navajo Lake at 10:00 A.M. in sun, pass by the opposite side of the lake where there are many nice campsites, and almost immediately begin to climb, gently, about 300 feet, until we reach the fork of the Woods Lake Trail, which goes off to the right. Here our path, which continues straight ahead, begins its descent of over 2,000 feet in about 2 miles through meadows filled with geranium and columbine, tall chiming bells and green gentian.

We look back toward the saddle. It is far from here. It belongs to some other life. Here in the meadow, stands of evergreen and aspen become dense woods. About ¾ mile from the Woods Lake Trail junction, another trail goes off the Navajo Lake Trail to the left (east, then south) to the Morgan Camp at The Meadows on the Dunton Road (see p. 137). Our path crosses the West Dolores via some slippery logs. I sit my way across one of them. The daily hailstorm begins. We put on raingear and take shelter under some evergreens. When the hail is over, we continue down the path, which ends about 4 miles from Navajo Lake, at a dirt road (parking) that leads to the improved dirt road to Dunton. Shortly after reaching this road we come to Burro Bridge Campground (a Forest Service campground with a nightly fee) and eat lunch at a table. This, I am forced to admit, does not feel bad.

We continue on the red dirt road, the West Dolores below us on our left, the hill above the river a mass of aspens, their quivering light green interspersed with the dark of evergreen. Wild roses grow along the red dirt roadside. After about 2 miles we come to Dunton.

Dunton was a mining town in the 1890s, a ghost town, a ranch, a dude ranch, and a hot-spring resort, in that order. It's the only town and the only bar in the valley. The main building is part of the

Dunton

original nineteenth-century town. The hot spring has been captured in a pool housed in an unpainted cabin. A ramshackle, friendly place, one can stay here overnight or longer comfortably, if simply, housed in gray plank cabins of varying sizes. Very large dogs lounge around in front of the bar, while people ride in and out of town on horseback. You may hire horses whether or not you are staying in Dunton.

We spend an hour in the bar, quite torn between going on with our hike or staying over in one of the cabins and taking up an offer of a ride to Telluride in the morning. In an attempt to make up our minds we ask directions to the Winter Trail. A crew went up yesterday to begin clearing it, we are told. It hasn't been used recently. By chance the head of the trail crew walks into the bar at this very moment. "It's hard to get through," he says.

"We can," we say. He sits down with us and goes over the

route on our map. But our decision was already made. We would be the first hikers on it in thirty years.

We leave Dunton on a dirt road above the corral, continue up about 1 mile, then turn onto a clearly discernible trail branching off the road to the left. We continue up this trail, through woods, across a meadow and a stream to a stand of pines on the edge of another meadow bordered by still another stream. A light rain has begun, and the pines make a good campsite on a wet evening, although the streams are too sluggish to be good sources of water. (Fill up with water at either Burro Bridge or Dunton.)

Lying in the tent listening to the light tapping of after-dinner rain, we look up to see a man on horseback approach. He is one of the trail crew, and we shout across the distance to each other. (His horse will not come closer to this tent that talks.) He describes the route across the meadows where there is no beaten path.

From the Winter Trail to the Highline Stock Drive—about 5 miles, about 3 hours

This morning is cloudy. All the other mornings have at least been brilliant and clear, whatever happened later. I have little wish to crawl out of the tent. Nevertheless, we manage to break camp by 8:15, cross the stream, and trudge upward through the high, wet grass of the long meadow. (Rain chaps are a salvation.) The ground, dug up by countless burrowing animals and the hooves of horses, is uneven and full of holes. Pushing through the grass is hard work, but the sun has, somewhat tentatively, appeared. The route continues northeast up the long meadow, heading into a U-shaped indentation in the aspen grove on the north side of the meadow. It continues up a ridge, climbing steeply for 400 feet, arriving at the lowest of three meadows. We climb the meadows heading east, staying on their north (left) side. The route continues northeast out of the third meadow, enters evergreen woods, following the 10,200-foot contour interval on the topo map. We struggle over countless blown-down trees, thirty years of blown-down trees. (The crew, of course, was up there to cut through them, so by publication date this should be an unobstructed path.) Mosquitos swarm around us. We come to the edge of a cliff, a rock outcropping dropping sharply away into a massive rubble of rock. Across the valley are superb views, including the isolated Lone Cone straight ahead and Lizard Head far to the right. (With all the intensity of the last few days I had completely forgotten about Lizard Head, but in fact it was always there. If we had ever become lost, we could never have gone far wrong by simply aiming for it.)

The trail follows the same contour about ¾ mile when it comes to a stream which runs eventually into Morrison Creek, which runs into the West Dolores. It crosses the stream and continues to the top of the escarpment, about another ½ mile, until it reaches a high, swampy, but beautiful meadow, the home of all the mosquitos on earth. They cover us in layers. Here the route crosses Morrison Creek and heads due east toward the clump of trees on the east side. Before reaching the trees we turn north, cross the open part of the meadow and a small creek, and soon pick up a jeep road which we follow the remainder of the way to The Meadows, the Morgan Camp, and the Dunton Road. We try to stay on the highest ground, although all of it is more or less marshy. This is the one point where the Winter Trail now diverges from the Winter Trail marked on the topo map. Once it has crossed Morrison Creek and turned north, it leads in almost a straight line to the Morgan Camp, while the old trail headed east and joined the Highline Stock Driveway somewhere in the marsh.

At the road the route turns right, continues about ¾ mile, crosses Coal Creek, and just afterward picks up the Highline (Groundhog) Stock Driveway on the left side of the road. It is marked with a sign and is a maintained path that covers about 6½ miles from The Meadows to Lizard Head Pass, which is about 1½ miles south of Trout Lake on Highway 145.

The sky has been darkening ever since we reached the meadow. Huge gray clouds roll in from the direction we have just come, and thunder rumbles in that distance. We reach the head of the Highline Stock Driveway and have just long enough to get our ponchos on—the rain has reached us—when up pulls a large station wagon from California. The driver makes us an offer we can't refuse. The three adults and three children had been fishing up near Dunton and rushed back to their car when the storm broke. We settle with our packs in a back corner on the carpeted floor and ride down the twisting red dirt road to 145 while the children watch us silently. We seem to be outrunning the rain, although no sooner do they leave us off on the highway than it begins in earnest. Miraculously, the first car to come our direction stops for us, and we jam ourselves and packs into what had been a dry Mustang. Our driver lets us off at Trout Lake, where we find my

Telluride

car. We look at one another, at how wet and muddy we are. We are impressed with our hitchhiking success. Like I said, it's a very relaxed state.

In Telluride we change out of our soaking boots and rush to the Floradora for a long and wonderful lunch.

/\/\/\

Before making this hike again, I would certainly consider supplications to various sun gods. Most of the route is only for experienced mountain hikers. For others, there are marvelous day hikes out of Telluride to abandoned mines and waterfalls, and the overnight trip to Navajo Lake from Burro Bridge Campground, the reverse of the route described on p. 134, is not difficult. Nor is the hike from Trout Lake up to Wilson Meadows, although the initial climb up from the lake is steep. In both cases the only way back to the starting point is by retracing the same route. At Navajo Lake, however, you have the option of hiking to the Woods Lake Trail to Silver Pick Basin and down to Bear Creek Road, from which you will have to hitch back to your car at Burro Bridge.

4 Grand Teton National Park, Wyoming—*From Teton Village to Jenny Lake*

I drove into Jackson, Wyoming, during a shoot-out. It happens nightly. The good guys shoot the bad guys and then everybody goes home. Jackson is a real cowboy town with covered board sidewalks, hitching posts, and silver-dollar bars. Mecca of my fantasies, the Wild West for which my soul yearned, I'd been aiming for it since childhood. At last, here I was, and not a cowboy in sight—nobody but throngs of families from all over America on their way to or from Yellowstone, trying on cowboy hats, watching shoot-outs arranged by the chamber of commerce, and looking for a place to eat.

I left and went directly to Teton Village, 12 miles from Jackson, set back along the edge of the mountains on the west side of Jackson Hole where the park begins. Looking out at the Gros Ventre across the vast, flat expanse of valley, carefully built to blend in with the mountains, full of every sort of pleasantness and amenity, Teton Village was a place I could simply have stayed—solace enough for having lost the West.

One of the attractions of the village is the tram ride up to the top of 10,450-foot Rendezvous Mountain. Susceptible to such attractions, I had planned to begin my hike via the tram. The northern section of the Tetons, where access is more difficult (see the Sierra Club Totebook *Hiking the Teton Backcountry*), is less crowded than this trip I had planned in the southern section. Even less crowded and just as beautiful are the trails of the Wind River Range (see books listed on pp. 146–47) and a good deal of the other backcountry areas of Wyoming. But I was eager to take advantage of some of the civilized amenities—restaurants, bars, swimming pools, shops, a concert hall, stables, etc. Teton Village, while "made up," is not unlike some European mountain villages, except that it has been placed next to some of the most gloriously wild country in America.

A LITTLE NATURAL HISTORY

The jagged, sky-piercing, snow-pocketed Tetons are among the youngest of the Rocky Mountains. On their eastern side they rise straight up from the flat land of Jackson Hole. No foothills soften their grandeur. White and wild water plunges down their steep sides, roaring into narrow canyons, down and down into the chain of lakes mirroring the mountains' power at their feet. Up high, small lakes glitter in the sun while fierce winds sweep across exposed ridges, shelves, and high passes stripped of everything but rock and buttercups. The dense forests of pine, spruce, and fir in the Transition and Canadian zones become dwarfed and wind-shaped higher up. In the meadows wild flowers bloom in orgiastic profusion. They are, quite simply, overwhelming.

So are the moose. There are lots of them. They may often be seen browsing by the rivers. Herds of elk and deer graze on the meadows at sunset. Marmots (some people call them rockchucks here) scamper everywhere. You may at least hear a coyote and possibly see fox, lynx, mink, wolverine, badger, beaver, otter, and probably some others. You will rarely see bears. There are over

200 kinds of birds, and you might spot an eagle or osprey in the branches of a dead tree.

The Tetons have an important social history. They, with the rest of Wyoming's mountains, were a focal point for the early trails to the Pacific Northwest. Among the major routes was the Snake River, which flows through Jackson Hole to join the Columbia. All the names connected with the opening of the West are here —Lewis and Clark, whose expedition discovered the Snake; John Colter, a member of that expedition who left it to trap on his own and discovered the Tetons, crossing them and the Wind River Range alone and on foot; the trapper Jim Bridger, the first white man to see the Great Salt Lake; the great mountain men like Jedediah Smith and William Sublette and all the others whose names are firmly imprinted in history books, on roadside markers, and in the names of mountains and flowers (like the Everts thistle, named for Truman C. Everts, a nineteenth-century explorer who got lost and lived on such thistles for thirty-seven days). It was French trappers who gave the Tetons their name, pronouncing the three most prominent points—the 13,770-foot Grand, 12,804-foot Middle, and 12,514-foot South Tetons—the "Trois Tetons" (three breasts). Rendezvous Mountain honors those historic meetings ("rendezvous") of the trappers, explorers, and fur companies where furs were sold, the mountain men resupplied, the news of America and the West relayed, and the men set up to go out again to their wild mountains.

CIVILIZED AMENITIES

Teton Village was constructed as a ski resort in 1965. It is expanding still. More lifts will be added while the carefully controlled town will grow. There is already something for everybody: accommodations ranging from $60.00 a day at the Hilton to $4.00 a day at the Hostel (both prices are per person, the Hostel's is based on four in a room), restaurants to suit every budget. By far the most popular of these is the Mangy Moose, whose long list of waiting diners (no reservations, give your name to the maitre d' when you arrive) sometimes ensures a wonderful wait of an hour or two in the bar. That it's worth it you can see by the numbers of people waiting in the bar. The Hilton and the Alpenhof have pools for their own guests, while guests at the rustic, friendly Hostel are invited to use the pool at the Sojourner. The Sojourner also offers a special daily rate for returning backpackers who don't want to overnight in a hotel but would like the luxury of a room for a day to clean up, nap, swim, etc. For $11.00 you may use a room from 9:00 A.M. to 6:00 P.M. and get two free cocktails as well. A coin laundry is available.

The most varied cuisine is offered by the Alpenhof, whose terrace is a marvelous spot for lunch. The village offers the possi- bility of horseback riding, bicycling, and raft trips down the Snake. There are numerous shops where you can fill in on backpacking, hiking, or climbing gear (although, in fact, you will have more va- riety of things in the shops in Jackson), a grocery, and liquor store. The Jackson Hole Mountain Guides, housed in the ski- school building, offer classes in rock climbing (all levels) and ice and snow techniques. Guide service is also available from them. For their brochure, write: Jackson Hole Mountain Guides, Teton Village, Wyoming 83025; (307) 733-4979.

The hub of the park is Jenny Lake, a great jumble of people and cars sprawled all over a small area on the southeastern shore of the lake. Here you will find a ranger station, general store (gro- ceries, toiletries, gifts, magazines, etc.), the Glen Exum climbing school, and Jenny Lake Campground, the smallest of the park's five campgrounds and restricted to tents and small camping vehicles.

Accommodations within the park range from the luxurious Jenny Lake Lodge, a little inland from the north shore of the lake, to the medium-priced Jackson Lake Lodge and the still less expen- sive cabins and tents of Colter Bay Village near Jackson Lake. The American Alpine Club maintains a climber's ranch 4 miles north cf Moose. For information, write: American Alpine Club, 113 East 90th Street, New York, New York 10028. The ranch phone (Wyoming) is (307) 733-4496.

Reservations at hotels are essential. Jenny Lake Lodge, for instance, is generally fully booked for August in January. Reservations may or may not be accepted for campgrounds within the park. (The park service has been experimenting with various systems.) The campgrounds, however, are always jammed. Try getting there early in the morning when most people leave. For information about park-operated campgrounds as well as other campgrounds and hotel accommodations both inside and outside the park, write: Grand Teton National Park, Moose, Wyoming 83012. For information about Jenny Lake and Jackson Lake lodges, and Colter Bay Village, write: Grand Teton Lodge Co., P.O. Box 240, Moran, Wyoming 83013. For accommodations in Teton Village, write: Teton Village Resort Association, Teton Village, Wyoming 83025.

Access to Jackson Hole is by car or by plane (Frontier Airlines). Each flight is met by a limousine that travels between the airport and Jackson Lake Lodge (and will let you off anywhere in between). There is also bus service three times daily for the 50-minute ride between Jackson and Jackson Lake Lodge, making intermediate stops on request ($3.95 one way). For schedule information: Grand Teton Lodge Co. There is a bus from the Wort Hotel in Jackson for the half-hour trip to Teton Village. Phone National Park Tours, (307) 733-4325, for the schedule. If you like trains, Amtrak goes to Rock Springs, 177 miles south of Jackson. There are buses between Rock Springs and Jackson.

SPECIAL REGULATIONS

Grand Teton National Park is crowded. People begin writing for backcountry reservations in January. If you want to count on making a trip of some days, you *must* have reservations. Permits may be picked up no sooner than 24 hours in advance of a hike. A certain percentage of the total backcountry capacity (half, as of this writing) is reservable; the rest is held for first come, first served. Nevertheless, no matter how early you get to the permit desk, unless you have reservations there is a good chance you will *not* get all the sites you would like. You might not get any. When I picked up my permit at the Moose Visitor Center the day before my hike, I overheard a man in front of me talking to the girl behind the permit desk.

"I'd like to make an overnight hike somewhere in the area tomorrow," he said. "Where can I go?"

She checked her list. "I'm sorry," she said. "The backcountry is completely booked for tomorrow."

Backcountry and capacity regulations change yearly. The capacity limits, which are for zones rather than specific campsites, do ensure that you will see relatively few other hikers. For reservations and backcountry information, write: Chief Ranger's Office, Grand Teton National Park, Moose, Wyoming 83012.

Anyone going substantially off-trail, or doing any technical climbing, *must* register with the Jenny Lake Ranger Station.

BOOKS AND MAPS

Hiking the Teton Backcountry, Paul Lawrence, published by the Sierra Club. Totebook, $4.95. A good and clear guide containing helpful information about weather and equipment and some natural history. He has numbered all campsites, but currently numbered campsites mean *only* firesites—zones are not, at present, numbered. Mr. Lawrence leads hikes throughout the Tetons. If you would like to have him as your guide, write to him, c/o Grand Teton Lodge Co., or check with the transportation desk at Jackson Lake Lodge.

Teton Trails, Bryan Harry, published by the Grand Teton Natural History Association. Paperback, $1.00. A small, efficient, and clear guide that is also inexpensive and lightweight.

Grand Teton National Park and Jackson's Hole, Orrin and Lorraine Bonney, published by Swallow Press. Paperback, $2.45. A great and confusing hodgepodge of information that attempts to serve as a guide to everything—roads, history, places, trails.

A Climber's Guide to the Teton Range, Leigh Ortenburger, published by the Sierra Club. Totebook, $3.95.

Grand Tetons—Wonderland for Boys and Girls, Lura D. Dickson, published by Dickson's, Inc., Seymour, Indiana. Paperback, $1.75.

Wind River Trails, Finis Mitchell, published by Wasatch Pub., Inc., Salt Lake City, Utah. Paperback, $2.95. Essential if there's no room in the Tetons.

Field Book: Wind River Range, Orrin and Lorraine Bonney, published by Swallow Press. Paperback, $4.95. Perhaps helpful in addition to the preceding book.

All of these books are available in shops in Jackson (the largest selection at Teton Mountaineering, Jackson, Wyoming 83001), most of them at the Moose Visitor Center or the store in Jenny Lake.

The USGS map, 15-minute series, "Grand Teton National Park," covers the whole area of the park as well as parts of Targhee National Forest and Teton National Forest. There are 7.5-minute quadrangles available as well.

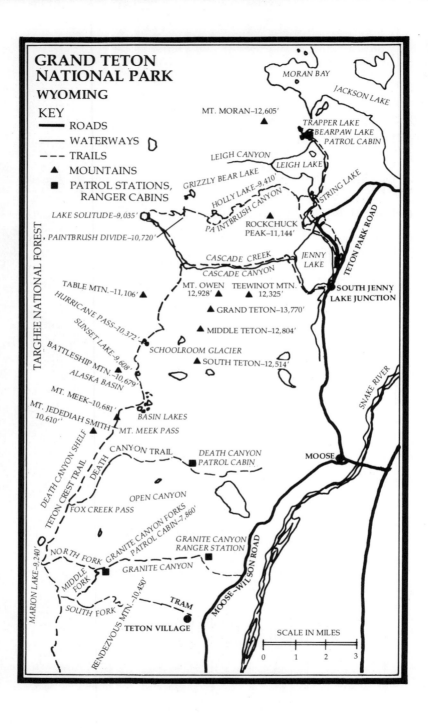

GRAND TETON
NATIONAL PARK
WYOMING

KEY
- ━━━ ROADS
- ──── WATERWAYS
- ----- TRAILS
- ▲ MOUNTAINS
- ■ PATROL STATIONS, RANGER CABINS

MORAN BAY

JACKSON LAKE

MT. MORAN–12,605'

TRAPPER LAKE
BEARPAW LAKE
PATROL CABIN

LEIGH CANYON

LEIGH LAKE

GRIZZLY BEAR LAKE

HOLLY LAKE–9,410'

STRING LAKE

LAKE SOLITUDE–9,035'

PAINTBRUSH CANYON

PAINTBRUSH DIVIDE–10,720'

ROCKCHUCK
PEAK–11,144'

TETON PARK ROAD

CASCADE CREEK

JENNY
LAKE

CASCADE CANYON

TARGHEE NATIONAL FOREST

TABLE MTN.–11,106' ▲

MT. OWEN
12,928' ▲

TEEWINOT MTN.
▲ 12,325'

SOUTH JENNY
LAKE JUNCTION

HURRICANE PASS–10,372'

▲ GRAND TETON–13,770'

SUNSET LAKE–9,608'

▲ MIDDLE TETON–12,804'

BATTLESHIP MTN.–10,679'

SCHOOLROOM GLACIER

ALASKA BASIN

▲ SOUTH TETON–12,514'

MT. MEEK–10,681'

BASIN LAKES

SNAKE RIVER

MT. JEDEDIAH SMITH
10,610''

MT. MEEK PASS

DEATH CANYON SHELF

CANYON TRAIL

DEATH CANYON
PATROL CABIN

MOOSE

TETON CREST TRAIL

DEATH

OPEN CANYON

FOX CREEK PASS

NORTH FORK

GRANITE CANYON FORKS
PATROL CABIN–7,860'

GRANITE CANYON
RANGER STATION

MARION LAKE–9,240'

MIDDLE
FORK

GRANITE CANYON

MOOSE–WILSON ROAD

SOUTH FORK

TRAM

RENDEZVOUS MTN.–10,450'

TETON VILLAGE

SCALE IN MILES

0   1   2   3

Teton Village/Rendezvous Mountain to
North Fork of Granite Canyon—6½ miles,
about 3 hours

It is a windy early morning in Teton Village and the Gros Ventre is hidden behind haze. Although it is the first part of August—the height of the tourist season—the line for the tram on such a day is not long. Even in the valley the wind's force seems to increase by the hour. The tram travels slower than usual as it rolls up its 2.4 miles from the village at 6,315 feet to the top of Rendezvous Mountain at 10,450 feet. We are greeted by 50-mile-an-hour gusts as we leave the tram. Now all of Jackson Hole also lies lost in haze, although it is nothing to ponder in that wind. It seems urgent to get off the tram platform and into the Crêperie as quickly as possible. Besides, the three of us are hungry.

The Crêperie is housed (as of this writing) in the old tram construction building, but a larger, "prettier" restaurant is planned for the spot. It's undoubtedly needed for the throngs of skiers in

Crêperie

winter, but I find tremendous appeal in the small space and very simple trappings of this one. I order a crêpe, pour myself a cup of coffee, sit down in a corner, and feel enormously happy, as if I had somehow gotten on an alp.

When we leave an hour later, I am wrapped in sweater, hat, and gloves against the powerful, cold wind that pierces through all my coverings anyway. We follow the path away from the tram, past the sign indicating Teton Village at the end of a long, steep trail on my left, toward the snowfields, then turn right (north) where the trail immediately descends into a large cirque, passing through stands of evergreens. To my right (northeast) the top of the 13,770-foot Grand Teton rises above everything.

Our trail continues, up now, into an open meadow filled with wild flowers, a thick, lush, vast field of wild flowers—white columbine, scarlet-red paintbrush, mauve geraniums, lupine, gentian, forget-me-nots; then again down through evergreens and out again, into flowering fields, the forests and fields alternating and the fields cut by

On top of Rendezvous Mountain

occasional streams of clear, rushing water; then ascending slightly to a meadow full of yellow senecios, mauve geraniums, purple-blue gentian, and others, endless others; dotted with stands of evergreens climbing up the green hills at the meadow's edge, guarded by gray-mauve scree slopes adorned with small, leftover patches of snow until it reaches the junction of the Middle Fork Cut-off, 3½ miles from the tram station.

The Middle Fork Cut-off leads west ½ mile to the Teton Crest Trail, along which it is 2.1 miles to Marion Lake. We remain on the Rendezvous Mountain Trail, which now enters the south fork of Granite Canyon and leads downhill through a meadow more spectacular than any of the others I have seen this morning—scarlet, purple, blue, bright yellow, sky blue, and mauve—all phenomenal colors I am not content to walk through but want to possess, to incorporate inside, to have, to see, to devour—Penthesilea devouring her lover—I pass through them unwillingly, yet knowing that even if I could stay in this meadow, the meadow would change. The colors would die. It is only because this year summer came so late that they are even now so vibrant—mere chance that I am passing through today.

The meadow becomes forest, but the flowers remain, still the scarlet paintbrush, the blue lupine, and now many more white columbine, a veritable orgy—what could be more masculine than lupine, or more feminine than columbine?

Continuing down through forest we come to North Fork Creek, cross it on the footbridge, then climb up to the Granite Canyon Forks Patrol Cabin at 7,860 feet. The trail swings (briefly) to the right. The paths you see directly ahead are cut-offs leading to the trail and bypassing the sign that assures you you are on the proper trail, which turns left (west) and continues upward. (To the right the trail leads back down Granite Canyon to the Granite Canyon Ranger Station and beyond it to the parking area and the Moose-Wilson Road.) Passing through more flowering meadows the trail comes, in less than a mile, to a large stand of pines next to the creek, North Fork. Here is flat, spacious camping space.

Shortly beyond that is a sign indicating Marion Lake, 1.8 miles away, and the junction of the Open Canyon Trail to the right (east). Following the trail upward, we find a few more good campsites on the left (near the creek).

We continue a short way past the sign, find a small (and by far not the best) campsite, and set up the tent. It is not yet 3:00, and I find myself a sunny rock for the afternoon. The grass and wild flowers surrounding me move gently in the cool breeze. I can hear North Fork Creek rushing away behind me. Myriad ants run rampant over the rock. Beyond the ants and me the rock cliffs rise up against a cloudless sky to the north, scattered stands of ever-greens climb the green hillside, white rock is strewn throughout the meadow painted with gold and purple, white, mauve, and blue —colors, no longer flowers but colors, spread themselves out across the meadow. It is quite a perfect place.

North Fork of Granite Canyon to Alaska
Basin—9.1 miles, about 5 hours

We leave camp at 9:30 A.M., cross the creek, and begin the climb up to Marion Lake (9,240 ft.) through woods and across open meadow. Half a mile on we come to the junction of the Teton Crest Trail (which we could have reached yesterday via the Middle Fork Cut-off). Here we turn right (north), pass a couple of good campsites, recross the creek, and continue upward, more steeply as the trail approaches Marion Lake. Marion Lake is idyllic, a gem. There is room here for a very few campers, and the site is generally booked far in advance. From the lake the trail continues upward, climbing in less than ½ mile to 9,550 feet, where it enters Targhee National Forest, then continues generally level to Fox Creek Pass, 2.3 miles beyond Marion Lake, where it reenters the park.

Looking west from the pass we have a view into Idaho. Here is the junction (at the pass, not in Idaho) of the Death Canyon Trail, which descends to the right (east and north). The Teton Crest Trail (which we will now follow for the next three days, runs

On the Teton Crest Trail

about 40 miles from Moose Creek Divide on the park's southern boundary to the String Lake parking area, near Jenny Lake) continues on the left, climbing up onto the Death Canyon Shelf, a rocky, wild flower-strewn open landscape with massive, vertical cliffs to the west. Death Canyon falls away at the eastern edge of this broad shelf. The canyon itself is deep with green meadows climbing up the shelf side and a forest of evergreens on the opposite side, its trail winding beautifully through it to come out 9.2 miles later at the White Grass Ranger Station.

The Teton Crest Trail, meanwhile, passes the ruins of an old trapper's cabin, the Grand always in view ahead as the trail leads 3 miles north to Mount Meek Pass (9,726 ft.), where it enters Targhee National Forest once more and continues down a short, steep switchback called the "sheep steps." Signs at both ends of the sheep steps advise caution. The steep and narrow trail goes over talus and snow, and footing could be slippery. At the bottom of the sheep steps the path enters Alaska Basin (9,550 ft.), a wide, glacier-scoured valley with some lovely lakes and many campsites. Since this is National Forest, there are not the same regulations in effect as in the other campsites on this route. Hence, there are many more people, although it is a large area and the boulders have so placed themselves that one is unaware of most of the other campers. Fires are allowed here.

We come to Teton Creek on the basin floor. It rushes past fast and cold and just too wide to jump. We walk quickly through to reach the lakes. Tomorrow's route begins on this side of the creek.

Alaska Basin to North Fork of Cascade Canyon—9.1 miles, about 5 hours

We leave Alaska Basin late, at 10:00, and head north, across the basin and up the switchback trail that climbs the steep first part of the mile up to Sunset Lake at 9,608 feet. The lake sits in a vast, open space hollowed out beneath great, treeless heights and windy passes. High up to the right (northeast) is a glimpse of the very top of the ever-present Grand. The long ribbon of trail over Hurricane Pass (10,372 ft.), 1.7 miles away, continues past the campsite where a large group of teenagers is breaking camp, past the lake where two bikini-clad girls dare the cold, clear water, then begins climbing in a series of switchbacks. From the lake the pass itself cannot be seen, but it is there; ahead, across, beyond the treeless, windswept mountain you walk on, which seems itself the top of the world, until suddenly the three Tetons erupt into view ahead on the right, and you understand there is no top to the world. They remain irrevocably, spectacularly in view until well into the descent down the Cascade Canyon South Fork.

At the top of the switchback the trail levels off as it leads across this rounded, stony, broad world. The wind increases as we

The trail from Sunset Lake to Hurricane Pass

near the pass, but with nowhere near the force of the last two days. I stop to put on my sweater, then continue to the gray, bare, rocky pass. The wind is strong and cold, yet nestled against a slight rise in the narrow pass, a father and small daughter have settled down to lunch. It is a spot worth the wind. To the east are views of the Tetons with the Schoolroom Glacier slightly to their southwest; to the west the massive, 10,679-foot Battleship Mountain; to the south, Mount Meek Pass over which we had come yesterday.

We walk past father and daughter and down a bit to a grassy ledge overlooking the Schoolroom Glacier. It, too, is an idyllic spot. Cascade Canyon lies far below, its deep-green grassy areas and evergreens, its gentle ribbon of a river a sharp contrast to the surroundings of this little oasis of a ledge—the jagged world of rock and snow from which water tumbles down in eternal tumult. The sun on the ledge is hot and we spend a lazy lunchtime before descending into the canyon via a series of switchbacks down this steeper side of the mountain.

The path occasionally crosses snow, finally comes out onto snow, passes stunted clumps of whitebark pine. Here the cascades falling sparkling down from the Tetons rush into white, tumbling water in the canyon. The sun is brilliant everywhere. Once in the canyon the trail levels off for a while, winds through stately white-bark pines, past wild flowers, always accompanied by the sound of water. A couple on their way up stops to talk. They are on their way from the North Fork to the end of the South Fork and had gone over Paintbrush Divide (tomorrow's trip) the day before.

"How was it?" I ask, having nervously read warnings in the guidebooks to check with Jenny Lake Ranger Station before starting out on it.

"Fine," the woman answers. "Steep, but fine. Your pack rubs against the snow on the side."

"I went across on my hands and knees," the man offers, laughing.

"He's afraid of heights," she explains. As she speaks, a mosquito lights on her bare arm.

"There's a mosquito on your arm," I mention.

"Yes. I know. I want to watch him bite," she says.

"Her," he says. "Only the females bite."

We circle around her to witness this event, which has taken on a great scientific importance. It bites her.

The canyon plunges away again and the path coils into another series of switchbacks, arriving, at the bottom, at a calm stretch of river that soon churns away once more as it goes over rapids. The trees change to spruce and fir. At 7,840 feet, a little over 5 miles from Alaska Basin, the trail reaches its junction with the North Fork Trail up to Lake Solitude (9,035 ft.), 2.7 miles away, and with the main trail down to Jenny Lake, 4½ miles away, and Jenny Lake Ranger Station, 2 miles farther on.

The North Fork Trail turns to the left (northwest), soon passing a ranger cabin, winds up through woods and over vast rock

Ranger cabin, North Fork of Cascade Canyon

slides. As we approach the wooden bridge over Cascade Creek, a marmot walks across it toward us, then disappears into the rocks. The path rises quickly high above the creek, whose gorge now lies deep on my right. The sun is hot and the path dry and dusty. With the creek below us, there is not much water now, although we come across one spring. We have been told there are not many good campsites along this route, but less than an hour past the ranger cabin we find a lovely one in a stand of evergreens below a babbling stream, a short way off the path to the right. Mount Owen, the Grand, and Teewinot Mountain provide a backdrop for the tent, and although the sun soon disappears from the clearing, it remains long on them and the mountains to the east.

North Fork of Cascade Canyon to Lower
Paintbrush Canyon—about 6 miles,
about 6 hours

No early sun finds its way into the deep and narrow north fork, although it is already strong on the eastern walls of Mount Owen and the Grand. In the gray morning cold I am glad to start moving and welcome a streak of sunlight falling on a talus slope we cross before returning into shadow. The path heads northwest up the canyon to Lake Solitude (9,035 ft.) in about ½ mile and from there along the northeast side of the lake until, leaving the lake, it turns to the right (east) as it begins the steep climb up the wall of the canyon to the snow-covered, 10,720-foot Paintbrush Divide. The 2.4 miles from the lake to the divide can take from 2 to 3 hours.

Every guidebook available issues a warning about the steep, slippery snowfield that often covers the trail from the divide to the first part of the descent into Paintbrush Canyon. In early summer, which in the case of late snow can continue for a long time, it is dangerous to attempt this route without an ice axe and the knowledge of how to use it. As I mentioned earlier, the guidebooks recommend checking with Jenny Lake Ranger Station before heading for the divide. But you do not come to Jenny Lake until *after* the divide if you follow this route, and there is no ranger along the way to ask. Check about its condition when you pick up your permit at Moose, although the person at the permit desk will automatically suggest an alternate route if it *is* dangerous.

We climb slowly up from the lake, finally reaching the snow and the flat ridge of the divide with its spectacular views; to the east of Gros Ventre and the Wind River Range; to the north of Leigh Canyon with Grizzly Bear Lake and beyond it of Mount Moran. Northeast we can see the immense Jackson Lake and, to the south, the Tetons, although concentrating on the path beneath my feet, I find I do not look much at the views. Still, the path is well trod and there is nothing dire about it. We bear left (north), continuing upward along the ridge a short ways. I do not feel insecure. When the narrow trail suddenly begins switchbacking steeply down toward Leigh Canyon Divide, the packs do rub against the snow. I dig my heels back into the snow with each step until all at once the snow is gone and the path no longer difficult. At this time the whole thing is far more difficult in reputation than in fact, and while I am pleased to be off the snow, I have to admit it was not bad at all.

We continue down to the right (southeast) in a series of switchbacks over huge, glacier-formed steps similar to the terrain down the south fork of Cascade Canyon. One and seven-tenths miles from the divide a trail branches off to the left (northeast) to Holly Lake (9,410 ft.), ½ mile from the main trail and a nice spot for lunch, although apt to be thronged with day hikers up from Jenny Lake—unless lunch is *very* early. The Holly Lake Trail rejoins the main trail farther down the canyon, shortcutting about ½ mile of the main trail, which continues down through forests of pine, fir, and spruce, and descends rapidly in switchbacks into the canyon. There is water everywhere as it roars and plunges through the rocky gorge and issues in springs along the side of the trail. Beneath the evergreens that stretch back from the trail there are a few luxurious spots to camp.

Lower Paintbrush Canyon to Trapper Lake—
about 7 miles, about 3½ hours

From the campsite in the pines we continue down the path through the forest. Two elk crash through the trees on our left. After about a 4-mile descent from the campsite, we arrive at the junction of the Leigh Lake cut-off, leading around the east shore of Leigh Lake to Bearpaw and Trapper lakes, while the main trail continues to the right to the south end of String Lake, to Jenny Lake, the road between the two lakes and the main road through the park. The cut-off leads directly east, coming in less than ½ mile to the bridge over the outlet to Leigh Lake. On our right is String Lake, which lies between Leigh and Jenny lakes. Over the bridge the trail rounds the southern end of Leigh Lake and exactly follows the east shore, 2.8 level miles to Bearpaw Lake.

This is all easy hiking, so there is plenty of time to while away some hours on the beach and in the cold, but clear, sparkling,

Leigh Lake

utterly inviting water of Leigh Lake. A sand beach exists about midway along the 2 miles of the lake. Across the lake both Leigh and Paintbrush canyons empty into it. So does water running off the glaciers of Mount Moran, high and mighty to the northwest.

The little island at the beginning of the lake is Boulder Island, the larger one near the end is Mystic Isle. A campsite is situated almost on the shore of Leigh Lake, and since it is so easy a walk there are many strollers back and forth all afternoon, but on an early sunny morning it is virtually one's own. At the north end of the lake is a ranger patrol cabin on the left. An abandoned trail from there continues around the end of the lake to Leigh Canyon, while our trail leaves the water and forest, crosses a broad, green meadow, reenters the forest, and then, ½ mile from Leigh Lake, comes to the beginning of pretty Bearpaw Lake nestled in a stand of evergreens. There is a nice campsite on its shore. Half a mile farther on is tiny Trapper Lake. Just past Bearpaw is a sign saying TRAIL NOT MAINTAINED, which means that nobody comes to cut the fallen trees, and that fewer people hike there altogether, most simply never going beyond Leigh Lake. But the trail, which goes around the western edge of Bearpaw Lake, is well defined and easy to follow. It climbs up slightly, away from the lake, still through woods, over and around many fallen trees (most of them small), and out into meadow again and the edge of Trapper Lake. There are two campsites to the right of the lake among the rocks. A stream runs down into the lake. The old, ill-defined, and largely un-used trail to Moran Bay on Jackson Lake crosses the stream and the large meadow on the opposite side of the lake.

You may build a fire (fire rings already exist) at all three of these lakes: Leigh, Bearpaw, and Trapper. At Bearpaw, and more so at Trapper, you will probably not see another soul.

Trapper Lake to Moose—
about 3.3 miles of trail and 10 miles of road,
about 1½ hours of walking

We wake to find a layer of frost covering everything. The sun is long in coming to this campsite, although it is halfway down the large sloping meadow on the other side of the lake, where two bull moose come out to graze. I envy them their sun. Shivering, we pack up and leave, coming upon a grazing elk in the meadow be-tween Bearpaw and Leigh lakes. We retrace our steps of yesterday, but instead of crossing the bridge at the end of Leigh Lake, we stay on the east side of the lake, headed toward the String Lake picnic area (parking), following the eastern shore of String Lake for about ¼ mile when we come to the junction of the trail to Jenny Lake Lodge.

Here we have a choice of several routes to South Jenny Lake Junction, where, if we are in time, I will be able to ride to Moose in the limousine that travels between Jackson Lake Lodge and the airport. (My companions are stopping at Jenny Lake.) There is a bus stop at the junction (although one should phone the transportation desk at Jackson Lake Lodge beforehand, both to make sure of the schedule and to announce one's presence. Phone: [307] 733-2811). From Moose I will have to hitch back to Teton Village.

Our choice of trails consists of (1) continuing on the road that runs from String Lake to South Jenny Lake Junction where it joins the main road, (2) continuing on a path along the east side of the lake and then along the east side of Jenny Lake to reach the road that joins the main road, or (3) simply staying on the trail through the meadow, past Jenny Lake Lodge. Thinking we might get a ride to the junction immediately, we follow the trail to the String Lake picnic area, but few cars are leaving at this early hour and we walk a mile before someone stops. Still, our ride gets us to the junction in time for me to board the limousine at 11:10 for the 15-minute ride to Moose. There is just room enough in it for me. When I get out the driver says, "I guess that's about seventy-five cents." I pull a dollar bill and a fifty-cent piece out of

The terrace of the
Alpenhof, lunchtime

my pocket. "I guess it's fifty cents," he says. "I haven't got time to make change."

At Moose (visitor center, ranger station, sporting-goods store, gas station, snack bar, and post office) I wait about 10 minutes before getting a ride directly into Teton Village, where I head immediately to the terrace of the Alpenhof for a lovely lunch of eggs benedict and white wine, and afterward, a swim in the pool of the Sojourner Inn.

/\/\/\

I would never just casually turn up in the Tetons expecting to backpack, but if I wanted to be in that region, I would make my reservations for campsites in January; decide on a holiday in Teton Village or at one of the lodges from where I could make day hikes; or investigate the Wind River Range. If I was able to get space in the Tetons and it was early in the season that extends from July through September, I would take an ice axe over Paintbrush Divide. Later on it is not necessary. (Don't carry one without knowing how to use it—it can be a fairly lethal weapon. You can learn how to use it by spending a day in snow school with the Jackson Hole Mountain Guides or Glen Exum Mountaineering School.)

It is possible to do this entire trip without the hike over Paintbrush Divide. It simply means retracing your steps—up and back—in both Cascade and Paintbrush canyons. It is also possible to make the hike and skip both canyons entirely, although that would be a great pity.

The combination of Grand Teton National Park and Teton Village might well serve as an example for other parks. The carefully planned and tastefully constructed village stands outside the park boundary, but offers easy access to the park. The only thing missing from its tourist services is a park visitor and information center. Obviously villages and parks have to plan together.

5   Isle Royale National Park, Michigan—*From Windigo to Rock Harbor*

Isle Royale is called the most wild of our National Parks because it is our only wholly roadless National Park. Its 200 square miles are cut by 165 miles of trails. The interior of the park can be reached only by foot or canoe, while travel between the island (actually, islands—Isle Royale is the largest of an archipelago of over 200 islands) and the mainland is by either boat or plane. It is a 2½-hour trip from Grand Portage, Minnesota, to Windigo; a 6-hour trip from Houghton, Michigan, to Rock Harbor; and a 4½-hour trip from Copper Harbor, Michigan, to Rock Harbor. The flight from Houghton to Rock Harbor takes ½ hour, and on the island, from Rock Harbor to Windigo a little less. The island belongs to Michigan, 50 miles to the southeast, because Michigan was the first of the territories in the Lake Superior area to be admitted to the U.S. But Minnesota, 18 miles to the west, is closer and more similar in its geology, geography, and biology. Minnesotans often assume it belongs to them.

In the late nineteenth and early twentieth centuries, when Isle Royale flourished as a health resort, hotels and private cot-

Fisherman's house

tages were more abundant. A large fishing industry, manned chiefly by Norwegians, fed the island as well as the mainland markets. A few of the old fishermen are left. So are a few private cottages whose owners hold lifetime leases on their property, which, since the founding of the National Park in 1940, cannot be renewed by the owners' heirs. The cottage of one of the old fishermen has become a tourist attraction. When the boat from Rock Harbor calls to deliver mail or groceries, all the passengers eagerly rush to the side for a glimpse into the life of this hardy old man. Private boats, too, call at his establishment, which with its old, weather-beaten wooden buildings is far more natural and alluring than the neatly manicured grounds of the park headquarters on Mott Island. (I don't suppose the park service could be expected to erect old shacks, but I wonder if they couldn't manage to look a bit less governmental.)

A LITTLE NATURAL HISTORY

The long, narrow main island is divided into parallel ridges and valleys, for the most part heavily forested except for a few extraordinary ridge crests of bare rock, magnificently open to that Great Lake, the largest body of fresh water in the world, over which they look. The forests in the interior are maple, birch, oak, and spruce-fir, predominantly maple on the northwestern end of the island. The maples give way to birch and spruce-fir as you head east. Near the lakes you find birch, aspen, pine, fir, and spruce. From every viewpoint you see evergreens interrupted by long, narrow lakes, and beyond all of it, Superior. The hilly terrain ranges from forest to bog and swamp, to open meadow and rocky shoreline, a variety that allows for an equally great variety cf wild flowers. Thimbleberry is ubiquitous. At times you must literally push your way through it.

The wildlife is unique and many people come to Isle Royale specifically because of it—because of the wolves, in the hope of seeing, or at least hearing, one. This is one of the few protected places in the U.S. where there are, indeed, any wolves left even to be protected. (As of this writing there is an attempt to change the status of the wolves in Minnesota from endangered to threatened, which means they could be hunted. In Alaska, the only other state where they still live, they are ruthlessly hunted.) Wolves of Isle Royale are shy and careful animals, rarely sighted by hikers. They arrived in the 1940s, traveling from the mainland on the winter ice. Once here, they found themselves a goodly number of moose who had swum over from Canada (Ontario, the nearest mainland, is 15 miles northwest of the southwest end of the island) in the early part of the century. While few people ever see a wolf, moose are very much in evidence. It is unlikely you will not see one on a hike. It is also unlikely you will not see a fox. Each campsite seems to have its own, which nonchalantly makes its rounds morning and evening. You must hang your food up at

Cow moose at breakfast

night, or if you plan to be away from camp fishing or hiking for a day. When the fox aren't after it, the squirrels will be. Beaver, snowshoe hare, and deer mice are common on the island. And there are, as well, otter, weasel, muskrat, bats, and probably a few others. The inland lakes are a veritable storehouse of northern pike, yellow perch, walleye, and brook trout.

It is possible to hike the length of the island in three or four days, but it is also possible to put together a much longer hike. Many people extend their days not to hike but to fish. Side trails extend off the two main ridge trails, the Greenstone and Minong. The Greenstone Ridge Trail, which extends 40 miles from Windigo to Rock Harbor, follows the island's highest points along its backbone and is the best-developed and most popular long trail. The Minong Ridge Trail, which more or less follows the western side of the island from Washington Harbor (near Windigo) 26 miles to McCargoe Cove, is largely unimproved (no bridges), is considered a more difficult trail because of that, and as a result, has many fewer hikers on it. Along this trail, particularly in the Todd Harbor area, one is far more likely than along the Greenstone Ridge Trail to see, or at least hear, a wolf.

CIVILIZED AMENITIES

I chose to start this hike from Minnesota and the Windigo Inn end of the island so I could spend my last night in the luxury of Rock Harbor Lodge, the only overnight commercial establishment left in the park. The guidebooks recommend hiking the Greenstone Ridge Trail (my route) the opposite way, from Rock Harbor to Windigo, because of the steep climb up from Windigo to Sugar Mountain. I am baffled by that. The 500-foot altitude difference between Windigo and Sugar Mountain happens gradually over 6 miles. It is difficult for me to imagine even a hiker from the prairie states experiencing that as a steep climb. Furthermore, it seemed to me that every downhill I encountered from Windigo to Rock Harbor (uphill coming the other way) was "steeper" than any uphill.

Isle Royale is accessible from Minnesota via Route 61, which follows the coast of Lake Superior from Duluth all the way up into Canada, 5 miles north of Grand Portage. There is once-a-day Greyhound bus service from Duluth to Grand Portage and back (see p. 41). The boat leaves from Grand Portage, established in 1731 as the first white settlement in Minnesota, home of the Voyageur, the Sioux, and later the Chippewa. It now consists of a post office, grocery, campground (behind the post office and grocery), a replica of a fort that was the center for that eighteenth-century community, the boat docks, and the spanking new and handsome Radisson Inn, owned by the Chippewa and managed by the Radisson Corporation. (Radisson hotels are named after the French explorer Pierre Radisson, who wandered about the north shore of Lake Superior in 1660, then went off to found the Hudson's Bay Company.) Very like the best of the new European hotels in flavor, except the art is Indian, it is not inexpensive. Rooms start at $26.00. For information and reservations, contact: Radisson Inn, Grand Portage, Minnesota 55605; (218) 475-2401. Located between Grand Marais, the largest town in the Grand Portage area, and Grand Portage is Naniboujou, originally a private club whose members included people like Babe Ruth and Jack Dempsey when it opened in 1929. It is a colorful, comfortable souvenir of another time. Rates are more reasonable than at the Radisson Inn. For information contact: Naniboujou, Grand Marais, Minnesota 55604; (218) 387-2688.

There are inns, lodges, cabins all the way up Route 61 from Duluth; some attractive, some seedy. Among the nicest is the lodge at Lutsen. About 90 minutes north of Duluth, it is too far from the dock to easily make the boat that leaves at 9:30 A.M., but its rustic comfort, soothing sauna, and pleasant dining room make it an ideal place to overnight on your way back from Isle Royale. For information, contact: Lutsen Resort, Lutsen, Minnesota 55612; (218) 663-7212.

One-way boat fare from Grand Portage to Windigo is $10.00 (round trip, $15.00). Grand Portage to Windigo, then Rock Harbor to Grand Portage, is $25.00. You should reserve ahead. For information, contact: Sivertson Brothers, 366 Lake Avenue South, Duluth, Minnesota 55802; (218) 722-0945. If you are coming from Houghton, Michigan, by boat, contact: Isle Royale National Park, P.O. Box 27, Houghton, Michigan 49931, Attention Ticket Teller; (906) 482-3310. From Houghton by plane: Isle Royale Seaplane Service, P.O. Box 371, Houghton, Michigan 49931. (The one-way air fare is only $7.00 more than the boat fare.) From Copper Harbor, Michigan, contact: Isle Royale Queen II, Copper Harbor, Michigan 49918; (906) 289-4437.

Rock Harbor Lodge is open from mid-June to Labor Day. Telephone: (906) 482-2890. Pre- and post-season, write: National Park Concessions, Inc., Mammoth Cave, Kentucky 42259. Rates include room and three meals. (If you won't be there for lunch, they'll pack one for you.) Two to a room, $45.00 per day.

At Rock Harbor there are sightseeing cruises, fishing trips, charter-boat service, boat rental (no canoes), and water-taxi service. You may bring a canoe over on the boat with you.

You can stock up with every sort of necessity in Grand Marais, which you pass through on your way to Grand Portage. There are several good stores for backpacking, hiking, and fishing supplies, among them the Lake Superior Trading Post, which carries everything from freeze-dried food and backpacks to moccasins and wild rice.

SPECIAL REGULATIONS

As of this writing there are no limitations on numbers of individual campers at each site. (The maximum group size is limited to 15.) Just the fact of being out in the middle of a Great Lake and having to arrive by boat or plane limits numbers to some extent, but not enough. Campsites, particularly along the Greenstone Ridge Trail and at both ends of the island, can be overcrowded enough to require doubling up. Eventually some sort of restrictions will undoubtedly be instituted.

You may camp at other than designated campsites and hike off the trails, but only after undergoing rigorous questioning by the rangers to determine if you are experienced enough to make such a trip. In that case, you *must* use a stove. Open fires are allowed only in the fire pits at designated campsites. But should you elect to go your own way, you will have some problems not generally encountered in off-trail hiking.

All water on Isle Royale (except that from the taps at Washington Creek, Rock Harbor, and Daisy Farm campgrounds) must be boiled at least five minutes. Halazone or other water purifiers will not work. Don't even bother carrying them. Only boiling will work to destroy the hydatid cysts in the island's water. Hydatid cysts infect the moose of Isle Royale, eating away their lungs over a course of about fifteen years. There are also known cases of the disease in humans. This means that if you are camping at other than designated sites, you must carry enough fuel with you to boil for five minutes every drop of water you use for drinking or cooking or brushing your teeth. For an overnight trip it doesn't amount to much. For four days or a week, it's a lot of fuel. But at designated campsites, almost every one of which is on a lake-shore, you may build fires to boil your water and cheer your soul.

Another thing about hiking off-trail on Isle Royale—it's full of bogs. The trails make an attempt to follow the highest ground, and where there *is* no highest ground, some bridges or boardwalks have been constructed, particularly along the Greenstone Ridge Trail. The bogs can make for some rather damp camping.

Even if you are not going off the trails or away from desig-nated campsites, it is still a good idea to carry a stove since rain is not uncommon here. But you must carry it across to the island without fuel. Coast-guard regulations do not allow transporting both combustible materials and passengers on the same boat. You may purchase small amounts of fuel (no need to buy a whole can) at both ends of the island, either at the shop in Rock Harbor or at the shop in the former dining room of the Windigo Inn. (The Windigo Inn itself was closed several years ago and probably will not reopen.)

Michigan and Minnesota are in different time zones, so if you ask someone the time, you might also ask which direction he's come from.

BOOKS AND MAPS

The Minnesota Walk Book, James W. Buchanan, published by the Sweetwater Press, Duluth. Paperback, $3.95.

Wilderness Trails—A Guide to the Trails in Isle Royale National Park, published by the Isle Royale Natural History Association. Paperback, 75¢.

The Wildflowers of Isle Royale, R. A. Janke and Nadine Janke, published by the Isle Royale Natural History Association. Paperback, $1.00.

The Wolves of Isle Royale, L. David Mech, published by the Government Printing Office, Washington, D.C. Paperback, $2.20.

Fishes and Sport Fishing in Isle Royale, K. F. Lagler and C. R. Goldman, published by the Isle Royale Natural History Association. Paperback, 60¢.

Forests and Trees of Isle Royale, R. M. Linn, published by the Isle Royale Natural History Association. Paperback, 60¢.

The Birds of Isle Royale, R. A. Janke, published by the Isle Royale Natural History Association. Paperback, 60¢.

The Life of Isle Royale, Napier Shelton, published by the National Park Service. Paperback, $3.30. An ecological handbook available from the Superintendent of Documents, U.S. Government Printing Office, Washington, D.C. 20402. Order stock number 024–005–00619–2. A check or money order must accompany the order.

These, plus a list of other books, are available from the Isle Royale Natural History Association, P.O. Box 27, Houghton, Michigan 49931. *The Minnesota Walk Book* is available at the Lake Superior Trading Post, Box 398, Grand Marais, Minnesota 55604.

There is a USGS topo map for Isle Royale, but more useful for seeing the whole island and trails with the addition of some capsule information is the large map of the island sold at the ranger and visitor stations for $1.00, "Isle Royale National Park, Michigan, Wilderness Trails."

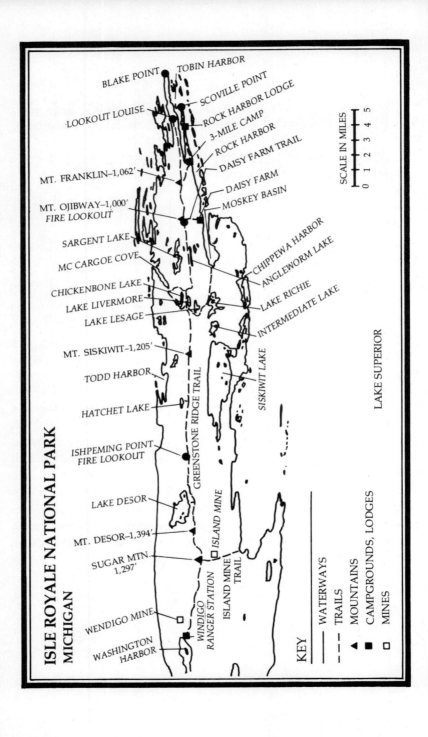

ISLE ROYALE NATIONAL PARK
MICHIGAN

TOBIN HARBOR

BLAKE POINT

SCOVILLE POINT

LOOKOUT LOUISE

ROCK HARBOR LODGE

3-MILE CAMP

ROCK HARBOR

DAISY FARM TRAIL

MT. FRANKLIN–1,062'

DAISY FARM

MT. OJIBWAY–1,000'
FIRE LOOKOUT

MOSKEY BASIN

SARGENT LAKE

CHIPPEWA HARBOR

MC CARGOE COVE

ANGLEWORM LAKE

CHICKENBONE LAKE

LAKE RICHIE

LAKE LIVERMORE

INTERMEDIATE LAKE

LAKE LESAGE

MT. SISKIWIT–1,205'

SISKIWIT LAKE

TODD HARBOR

LAKE SUPERIOR

HATCHET LAKE

GREENSTONE RIDGE TRAIL

ISHPEMING POINT
FIRE LOOKOUT

LAKE DESOR

ISLAND MINE

MT. DESOR–1,394'

ISLAND MINE TRAIL

SUGAR MTN.
1,297'

WINDIGO RANGER STATION

WENDIGO MINE

WASHINGTON HARBOR

SCALE IN MILES
0 1 2 3 4 5

KEY

—— WATERWAYS
- - - TRAILS
▲ MOUNTAINS
■ CAMPGROUNDS, LODGES
□ MINES

Grand Portage to Windigo—
2½ hours by boat

Five minutes after the warning blast that resounds throughout Grand Portage, the Wenonah puts out at 9:30 (Minnesota time) in the clear August morning. The boat is full, the mass of backpacks fed into a hold below deck, the overflow contained in a large cage on the aft deck. Embarking in sun, we head directly into fog that quickly envelops both the boat and the world. A little over 2 hours later the fog lifts enough for us to see the first of some smaller islands in the Isle Royale archipelago. In less than ½ hour we land at Windigo. A ranger meets the boat, asks all the day visitors to go to the water end of the dock, the backpackers and campers to form a group at the land end. We form a circle around him. It smacks a bit of summer camp, but is probably the only efficient way of disseminating information in a place where *all* the day's visitors arrive at exactly the same moment. He tells us everything we need to know—the water pump is broken, permits are issued in the ranger station, we should not get between a cow moose and her calf, etc., etc. Backpacks are scattered everywhere: on the dock, on the path leading to the dock, against the path's embankment, leaning against the ranger station, the signposts, boulders, each other. An enormous group of people sits, stands, lies, sleeps —strewn in as haphazard a manner as the packs—waiting to return to the mainland when the boat leaves at 3:00 (Michigan time)—surely some strange group of refugees awaiting evacuation.

The newly arrived hikers are clean, their faces glowing with anticipation. The ranger station is jammed with them. One of each new group crowds around the desk to get a permit, purchase maps, ask questions. It takes about an hour before the new arrivals are ready to begin their various journeys. Those heading for the campground a few minutes away get off first, followed by the eager, but motley, group of backpackers.

Windigo to Island Mine—
6¼ miles, about 3 hours

The Greenstone Ridge Trail leaves the harbor, passes the Windigo Campground, forks to the right (east), and enters a forest of maple trees. No sooner are we past the campground when I frighten a cow moose and her calf browsing in the path. They crash into the woods on the right, I jump slightly back. Venturing forward again, I find them about 10 feet in from the trail, their backs turned toward it, their necks craning around to see what will happen next. We continue quickly by. The trail climbs gradually from a little over 600 feet at the ranger station (Lake Superior is 602.3 feet above sea level) on its way to Sugar Mountain (1,297 ft.). The fog that absorbed us on the lake seeps through the forest, closes us in. Isle Royale weather can be very wet. I try not to think about it, although it is difficult to think about anything else.

On top of Sugar Mountain we come to the junction of the Island Mine Trail to the right, the path to tonight's campsite. Following it, we go first downhill, then up, coming in about ¼ mile to the first of the campsites which are scattered in clearings throughout the area. Each site has a fire pit, although this late in the season (August) there is no water nearby. Earlier there is supposed to be some if you continue on the Island Mine Trail past the group campsite to a spring. In any case, you can get water at Windigo to carry to this site, and for the rest of the trip water is available from the lakes.

As we sit talking after dinner around our roaring fire a fox comes to watch. He stands a little away from us, then walks slowly off, around the back of the tents and through the woods.

Island Mine to Lake Desor to Hatchet Lake—
12.3 miles, about 6 hours

Somewhere up there above the trees the morning dawns clear. I still feel closed in by the forest, but at least the humid grayness is gone. As is the case with most campsites here, we must begin by retracing our steps back to the main trail. The Island Mine Trail leads quickly away from camp, first down, then up and back to the main trail, which proceeds gently up over the top of 1,394-foot Mount Desor, the highest point on the island. Shortly after Mount Desor the trail—at last—breaks out of the maple forest and into the open, the sun, the sky! To the left is the first view of Lake Desor and beyond it of Lake Superior and Canada. From Mount Desor the trail winds in and out of birch forest and open, sunny places, descending all the while to the junction of the trail to the Lake Desor Campsite, 5.2 miles from the Island Mine Trail junction.

We had started at 7:45 to arrive at the lake at 10:15, where we boil enough water for the rest of the hike to Hatchet Lake. At that hour, if we had wanted to stay at Lake Desor, we could have our choice of lakeshore campsites, but we climb back up to the trail, which continues gently up and down and level as it passes through high ferns and thimbleberry, through birch forest and across meadows where the hot sun has turned the leaves to yellow. Pearly everlasting and big-leafed asters stand out among all the green and yellow. Off each side of the ridge are views of Lake Superior and, for the first time, I have a real sense of being on an island. A little over 3 miles from Lake Desor the trail leads to Ishpeming Point fire tower located on top of the second-highest hill on the island. (Don't ask the rangers at fire towers for water— they haven't got much.)

After Ishpeming Point the thimbleberries along the trail are high and thick and I virtually push my way through them, convinced no one has traveled this trail in months, although when I look down at the trail it is always clearly defined beneath my feet. (If only I *liked* thimbleberries—what a feast!) Shortly past Ishpeming Point I surprise a moose munching leaves next to the trail. We both, rather rapidly, go our own ways. Mine passes through a birch forest of extraordinary beauty, then over rock where the trail is marked by cairns. About an hour from the fire tower, halfway between Ishpeming Point and Hatchet Lake, is a viewpoint to the left (marked with a sign) that makes a nice rest stop and offers views of Hatchet Lake and Superior to the northeast, Siskiwit Lake and Superior on the opposite side of the island to the southeast.

A little before the junction of the Greenstone Ridge Trail and Hatchet Lake Trail there is another view of Hatchet Lake off to the left. The Hatchet Lake Trail goes steeply down to the lake, where there is a shelter and a number of individual and group sites. It's filled early with hikers coming from the opposite direction, so one may have to search a bit for a campsite. It is not uncommon on Isle Royale for people to have to share campsites.

Hatchet Lake to Chickenbone Lake—
7 miles, 3½ hours

Two fox walk through camp this morning, going in opposite directions. We leave Hatchet Lake at 8:30, climb 300 feet in ¼ mile back up to the ridge, then begin again, in bright sun, under a cloudless blue sky. The trail almost immediately enters woods but, wonderfully, the thimbleberries are less obtrusive than they have been until now, and after about an hour the path comes out into open space as it approaches Mount Siskiwit (1,205 ft.). How joyous each opening on this route makes me! (For sure, nowhere in my past could I have been a forest dweller.) From Mount Siskiwit there are views of Siskiwit Lake, the largest lake on the island, of Intermediate Lake and Siskiwit Bay to the right (south), and of Chickenbone, almost straight ahead to the east. (It's called "Chickenbone" because of its shape, but I somehow dreaded reaching it since in my imagination its entire shore was ringed with discarded chicken bones.) Just south of Chickenbone you can see Lakes Livermore, LeSage, and Richie, while north of Chickenbone is McCargoe Cove where a large settlement flourished in the 1870s, its life based on the operation of the largest of Isle Royale's many copper mines, the Minong Mine. The only thing left of the community is its space, which is currently a campsite (Lakeside Camp). There are a few remnants of the mining operation at the mine site. Since McCargoe Cove is only 2.2 miles from the Greenstone Ridge, it can make a nice side trip from Chickenbone Camp.

Mount Siskiwit is about halfway between Hatchet Lake and Chickenbone. About 2¾ hours past Hatchet Lake the trail begins its descent to Chickenbone Lake, steeply at the very top (this is, in fact, the steepest terrain along the Greenstone Ridge Trail, but it is not long), then more gently, sometimes leveling out as it passes through forest, along the hillside, down and across a stream (or somewhat swampy area, depending on what time of summer you hike) to the junction of the trail to McCargoe Cove on the left and Lake Richie, Moskey Basin, and Chippewa Harbor on the right. From here it is a steep 0.2 mile to the campsite on the lake.

We arrive at Chickenbone Lake early, after a stop on Mount Siskiwit for lunch, and have our choice of sites and the luxury of an entire afternoon to boil water and hike to McCargoe Cove.

Chickenbone Lake to 3-Mile Camp—
11½ miles, 5¾ hours

We leave Chickenbone Lake at 8:30. The climb up seems less steep than it had going down. The path leads through woods, past Lake Livermore (guaranteed good fishing, I understand; our nearest neighbors last night had three very large fish for dinner), generally level until it begins the climb back up out of the break in the Greenstone Ridge that had begun just after Mount Siskiwit, and out again, into the open. It remains mainly open, passing through an occasional woods, all the way to Mount Franklin. Again there are spectacular views off both sides of the ridge, toward Canada on the left and Michigan on the right. After walking 5.8 miles we come to the junction of a trail to Daisy Farm, the largest and most popular campsite on the island and one, like those at Windigo and Rock Harbor, where filtered water comes out of a tap. The

Afternoon at the lake

Daisy Farm Trail turns right while our trail to Mount Ojibway continues straight ahead.

The approach to Mount Ojibway and its fire tower is over lovely meadow. An occasional tree stands up from the hillside. The trail climbs gently, descends, then climbs easily again to the tower, 7.2 miles from Chickenbone. From the top of the tower you can see Sargent and Angleworm lakes to the west, but Chickenbone is blocked by the ridge between Sargent and it. You can see *almost* around the eastern end of the island. Leaving Ojibway, you have a choice of several trails. You can head south the 2 miles to Daisy Farm or continue east on the Greenstone Ridge, 2.5 miles to Mount Franklin and from there 5 miles farther to Lookout Louise at the northeastern terminus of the Greenstone Ridge Trail. From here you can descend almost a mile to Tobin Harbor, but you end up *across* the harbor from the Rock Harbor Lodge and Visitor Center, and unless you have somehow made an arrangement with a water taxi to pick you up here (which you can do through the Rock Harbor Lodge), you will have to retrace your steps to Mount Franklin. Just before you come to Tobin Harbor you pass Hidden Lake, an area of abundant wildlife, including wolves. There is no campground here. You can also go (as this route does) from Mount Franklin to 3-Mile Camp, 2 miles southeast.

Mount Franklin is not marked, but it is unmistakable. Past Mount Ojibway the trail climbs gently up into and across a lovely meadow, descends, then climbs gradually up again to reach some red rocks on your left. This is Mount Franklin. The red rocks are unlike anything else around. There are superb views here of Canada. Shortly past Mount Franklin you come to the junction of the trail to 3-Mile Camp. Turn right, descend steeply the first few feet. The trail gentles, then levels out as it passes through vast fields of thimbleberries followed by birch forest. After 1½ miles it reaches the junction of the Tobin Harbor Trail to Rock Harbor, off to the left. Three-Mile Camp is straight ahead, over a couple of very long plank bridges across swampland and a stream, then up a little as the path arrives at the first of the group sites and, continuing on to the shore of Lake Superior, comes to the individual sites, all with grills and picnic tables. There are a number of shelters here as well, a large boat dock, a chest full of bags of charcoal (25¢ a bag at this writing —honor system), and a goodly number of seagulls. It is quite wonderful to lie in the late afternoon sun on the dock.

People begin arriving in droves between 3:00 and 4:30 from the boat docking in Rock Harbor about 1:00. Time your hike to get there before that or you'll never find a campsite. The shelters are all taken early by people who have come up from Rock Harbor Campsite early in the day. The site on the lake is beautiful and almost worth putting up with the atmosphere created by the shelters, grills, and garbage cans.

With my companions in a nearby site, I set up my tent in a tiny site next to the water—there is just room enough for the tent to fit and for me to still get in and out of it—then set water on to boil. As we sit down to dinner we hear a woman shouting from somewhere down the boardwalk that runs through the low, damp ground of the camp.

"Bob, there's a large moose on the boardwalk! Don't let the children get too near!"

People have such odd senses of humor, I think, as I go on about my dinner. During dessert, the ranger, who has arrived by boat for his nightly visit, stops by. "Did you see the moose?" he asks.

"You mean there really was one?" It seems so unlikely to me that a moose would be walking up and down a boardwalk in so settled a place. (In fact, she was not *on* the boardwalk, but alongside it. Moose won't walk on boardwalks.)

"Yes, I circled around behind the shelters," he says. "I don't want to run into her."

The ranger continues on his way to the next campsite and I, having recently become very sophisticated about moose, no longer think about it. We sit by the fire until the sun is down, then crawl into our tents and sleeping bags and fall asleep.

Two hours later there is a suspiciously familiar crashing at the back of the tent. I look out in time to see the moose, a cow, just coming around to the front of the tent and then into the woods directly in front where she begins browsing. And moaning. Each few seconds of chomping is followed by a low moan. It is the only sound in this night, brilliantly lit by the full moon. I leave the tent and sit on the picnic table, convinced if she comes back she must either trip over the tent strings (which I cannot imagine how she had avoided in the first place) or walk into the tent altogether, the space is so tiny here and the moose both so nearsighted and so large. Besides, she is obviously sick and probably isn't paying much attention to what she's doing. But moaning, she moves off deeper into the woods, and although I can still hear her, I feel she has definitely headed away and I'm cold. I crawl back into the tent and listen to her moaning, and when I can no longer hear her I fall asleep.

At 2:00 A.M. she returns. Her footsteps jolt me immediately awake. She circles the tent again, close behind, then goes to browse between the tent and the lake, another small space. Her stomach-ache (my diagnosis) seems to be over, and I lie there listening to her munching. I do not hear her move off, although there is a sudden great clatter at the next campsite where something other than a moose has discovered, and is now licking and scattering, all the dishes and pots that must have been left on their table. For some reason the noise does not seem to affect the people camping there, who never make a sound or move to end it. Abruptly there is silence. Then, in the distance, a loon begins to cry.

3-Mile Camp to Rock Harbor—
3 miles, 1½ hours

The trail leaves camp along the shore, passing the dock and continuing mainly over the rocky outcroppings that edge the lake, occasionally passing through woods, undulating all the way as it crosses stones and rock, earth and tree stumps. The Ranger III passes on its way from Rock Harbor to Houghton. A family of ducks swims close in to the shore. The sun is brilliant and hot, the water laps gently against the rock. I have a great sense of being on an island in a powerful sea. After about 1½ miles people begin to appear from the Rock Harbor direction. At 2.9 miles we arrive at Rock Harbor, passing first through the campgrounds, then coming to the visitor center and harbor. There is a great bustle here. It is a busy small harbor. Boats are moored along the quay and people amble back and forth between the Rock Harbor Lodge and the store and visitor center.

The store is well stocked (including freeze-dried food). There are showers (towel and soap provided) and a Laundromat.

We head toward the lodge where we have reservations (essential) and go off to a room overlooking the white-capped lake, to shower before lunch. Meals in the busy dining room are simple, American fare served in a friendly atmosphere. You may eat there even if you are not staying at the lodge. Next door to the dining room are a coffee shop and gift shop.

In the afternoon we have time for the 5-mile walk on the trail to Scoville Point, 2.3 miles from the lodge around one of the eastern ends of the island. (The *most* eastern end, Blake Point, extends out beyond Lookout Louise on another finger of the island. There are no paths to it, although there is a campground [Merritt's Lane] accessible by boat.) There is a free guide to the Scoville Point Trail (actually, the Albert Stoll, Jr., Memorial Trail), which you can pick up at the visitor center and which is worth having a look at. With or without the guide, this is a scenic trail that provides a great and powerful sense of being on a high, rocky, windy island. Here, at last, I feel the force of this great lake, of the isolation of this island, of some wild, primitive nature. It is what I had looked for all along.

Rock Harbor

Lake Superior

Viewed by prairie-state standards, Isle Royale has lots of ups and downs. The island is indeed hilly, although anyone used to hiking in either eastern or western mountains will probably notice only that the trail goes gently up and down, but seems mainly level. But because it is not overtly mountainous, the island attracts many new backpackers. I think it's a fine place to begin—providing you are already an experienced hiker. There is no place here to simply retrace your steps to some nearby road and get out if your feet blister, or you change your mind about the whole thing. On the boat from Grand Portage I saw more new hiking boots than I've seen in a shop. Since only a new hiker would wear new boots on a backpacking trip, I wondered a good deal how they would all feel two days later. I did see, on the following day, one unhappy young man come limping into the Lake Desor Campsite, his pack being carried by his friends. While it may be an ideal place to begin backpacking, it is no place, because of its isolation, to begin hiking *and* backpacking.

6 Great Smoky Mountains National Park, Tennessee-North Carolina—*A circular journey, beginning and ending in Cataloochee*

The mountains do smoke. In the morning a deep-blue haze hovers over their dark shapes, which stretch 71 miles along the Tennessee–North Carolina border. This is the western escarpment of the Appalachians. They merge in the east with the Blue Ridge. It is a special world of giant trees; spectacular displays of mountain laurel and rhododendron. It is a jumble of moss-covered ancient logs rotting into earth; the white, stark, huge limbs of long-dead chestnut trees, their trunks swirled about as they soar skyward; deep, glistening wood sorrel; dark violets. With a sudden fluttering of great wings an owl lights in a tree beside the trail, watching, waiting, finally lifting himself, soaring, to a farther tree. A junco flitters up from the side of the path. There, where the grass or moss or roots or mud hangs over to form a roof, he's built his nest. Three white eggs lie nestled in it. A salamander slithers out of the inside of a log, then disappears under it. A mouse runs across the path; a boar roots around the front of a shelter; a rabbit munches grass in a gentle clearing; a million lives are here.

A LITTLE NATURAL HISTORY

The heavily forested Smokies include the third-highest peak in the East, the 6,642-foot Clingmans Dome. There are 15 other peaks higher than 6,000 feet. Over 650 miles of trails, of which 68 are part of the Appalachian Trail, lace the park. Besides boars and salamanders (including one—the red-cheeked salamander—endemic to the park) and over 200 different kinds of birds, there are bears, deer, squirrels, skunks, opossums, raccoons, bobcats, fox, a few other small, furry things. While seldom seen, there are also copperheads and rattlesnakes. (It's a good idea to look before placing your hand on a rock or log.)

The weather in the Smokies is wet. It's the wettest place in the U.S. besides the Pacific Northwest. The average annual rainfall can be more than 90 inches at altitudes above 6,000 feet. I have no doubt that at least 86 of those inches fell while I was hiking there one May. Good raingear and a stove are essential. Fires are permitted at authorized campsites, but because of the weather, they may never be possible. The Smokies have a long summer hiking season, April through October, but it does get cold, with the winter climate approaching perfect conditions for hypothermia.

Odd and varied names exist here. One trail or area can (and usually does) have more than one name. The people who lived in these mountains, for so long isolated, developed (or maintained) a rich and descriptive language. Words for things often have nothing to do with the words hikers are used to for things. *Knob,* for instance, means peak. A *bald* is a grassy mountaintop devoid of trees (but not above timberline, which would be about 10,000 feet here), or a *bald* can be a *slick* (also called a *woolly patch*), which is a tangle of low rhododendron or laurel. Laurel itself is called *mountain ivy,* while rhododendron is called laurel. *Forks* and *prongs* are waterways. A *lead* is a long ridge connecting two mountains. You'll come across other wonderful words and some rather fanciful names for places.

CIVILIZED AMENITIES

The park has two main visitor centers. The Sugarlands Visitor Center and Park Headquarters are 2 miles south of Gatlinburg, Tennessee, a lively, attractive resort town filled with restaurants, lodging, shops (including the handsome Arrowcraft Shop, an outlet for native crafts—weaving, carving, basketry, etc.). Gatlinburg is by far the most varied and interesting of the towns surrounding the park. For information about lodging there, write: Chamber of Commerce, Gatlinburg, Tennessee 37738. Sugarlands provides access to some of the most crowded areas of the park, including a variety of trails to the 6,593-foot Mount Le Conte and Le Conte Lodge which sits a bit below the summit. The unique rustic lodge and its cabins with wood-

*A quiet trail in
Cataloochie*

burning fireplaces can be reached only by foot or by horse and makes a nice stopover on a backpacking trip. Rates of $15.00 for adults and $11.00 for children 10 or under (as of this writing) plus tax and gratuities include bed, breakfast, and dinner. Meals are family-style. You get a $1.50 discount if you use your sleeping bag instead of their sheets. Reservations are essential. Write: Le Conte Lodge, P.O. Box 350, Gatlinburg, Tennessee 37738; or telephone: (615) 436-4473, weekdays 9:00 to 4:00. It would be possible to connect a tour in Cataloochee with trails leading to the lodge and ultimately to roads to Gatlinburg.

To the south of the park is the Cherokee Indian Reservation and the town of Cherokee, which seems hardly more than a honky-tonk crossroads, although the Indians do own and run a pleasant motel nearby, the Boundary Tree Motor Lodge. There is also a Holiday Inn operated by two Cherokee brothers near the center of town. (Further information is available from the motels themselves, Cherokee, North Carolina.) Near the reservation is the main North Carolina entrance to the park. Here, at Oconaluftee, an entire pioneer farmstead has been preserved as a museum. It's nicely done and provides insight into what life used to be like in this area before the advent of National Parks and backpackers. The Blue Ridge Parkway passes close to this entrance, connecting the Smokies to Shenandoah National Park in Virginia via a highly scenic route. Other accommodations are available in nearby areas like Bryson City and Maggie Valley. Information is available from the Travel and Promotion Division, Department of Natural and Economic Resources, Raleigh, North Carolina 27611.

North of the park, in Newport, Tennessee, the W. C. Hochstetlers (Waterville Star Route, Newport, Tennessee 37821) can provide you with overnight accommodations and home cooking. But even more important, Mr. Hochstetler maintains a shuttle service. He will go with you to your starting point anywhere in the park, then take your car to his house where it is safe, and meet you again at the end of your hike. His rates, which he hasn't raised in fifteen years, are per vehicle. All arrangements must be made by mail and you should include dates and locations of your hike's start and finish. Make arrangements as far in advance as possible to ensure he has the dates open.

Partly because of its long season, and partly because it is an eastern park fairly near many large metropolitan areas, Great Smoky Mountains National Park is the most visited of all our National Parks. Traffic moves slowly on the Newfound Gap Road, which passes through the park from the main North Carolina entrance to the main Tennessee entrance. Sometimes traffic doesn't move at all. Those campsites a short walk in from dirt roads are heavily used. So are many trails, particularly in the area around Clingmans Dome. The Appalachian Trail, it virtually goes without saying, is thronged. But less-used parts of the park, both early and late in the season (i.e., May, October), are free of crowds. In Cataloochee in May we didn't see another person for two days, until we neared the Appalachian Trail.

SPECIAL REGULATIONS

Backcountry permits can be obtained at the visitor centers and all ranger stations, or, for nonrationed areas, by mail no more than 30 days in advance. Rationed areas include all the shelters on the Appalachian Trail and those at Mount Le Conte, Kephart Prong, Laurel Gap, and Moore Spring. In these places campers are limited to the capacity of each shelter (12 to 14 people) and tenting is not allowed in the vicinity. As of this writing permits for rationed areas must be requested in person not more than 24 hours before the beginning of your hike, but since regulations change fairly often, it would be wise to inquire about current rules. Write: Park Superintendent, Great Smoky Mountains National Park, Gatlinburg, Tennessee 37738. For winter camping, permits are issued only after a ranger has inspected (and found adequate) all clothing and equipment.

BOOKS AND MAPS

Hikers' Guide to the Smokies, Dick Murlless and Constance Stallings, published by the Sierra Club. Totebook, $7.95. A complete, clear guidebook, thick with information about trails, flora and fauna, history, weather, etc., and a bibliography of books on the Smokies. It also contains the best map for the region.

Appalachian Hiker, Edward Garvey, published by Appalachian Books. Paperback, $4.50.

Guide to the Appalachian Trail in the Great Smokies, The Nantahalas, and Georgia, Appalachian Trail Conference, $6.00.

Guide to the Appalachian Trail in Tennessee and North Carolina, Appalachian Trail Conference, $6.00.

Appalachian Wilderness, photos by Eliot Porter, text by Edward Abbey, published by Ballantine Books. Oversized paperback, $4.95. A beautiful book whose photographs simply envelop one in the Smokies.

There are a great many books about the natural and social history of the park. A list (and the books) is available from: Great Smoky Mountains Natural History Association, Gatlinburg, Tennessee 37738. Books and maps are also available at the visitor centers.

Besides the map in the *Hikers' Guide to the Smokies,* which is also available in both paper and plastic from the Sierra Club, without the book, there are several USGS maps. The 15-minute series includes two maps—"Great Smoky Mountains National Park, Tennessee and North Carolina, East Half"; and its companion, the "West Half." These maps date from 1931 and all trails are not shown on them. Quadrangles for the entire park are available in 7.5-minute series and a more recent, but still not entirely up-to-date map for the entire park, "Great Smoky Mountains National Park and Vicinity," is scaled at 1:125,000. A map showing 100 favorite trails of the Great Smokies and Carolina Blue Ridge, compiled by the Carolina Mountain Club and the Smoky Mountains Hiking Club, sells for $1.00 and includes descriptive text and information about campsites. It is available from: The Stephens Press, Inc., Box 5655, Asheville, North Carolina 28803.

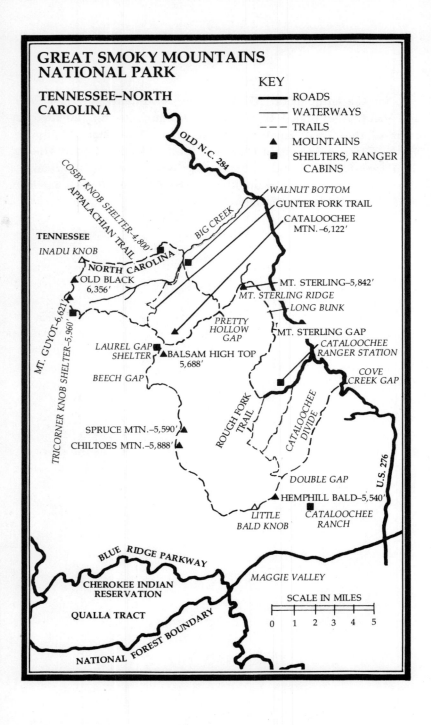

Cataloochee Divide, Cove Creek Gap to
Double Gap—6.2 miles, 3 hours

It was raining when we drove into the Smokies. It began raining in the cool, spring morning when we left Virginia and rained harder and harder as we drove through hilly, deep-green farmland. Interstate 40 bisects the broad valley through which we drove, dividing the villages on the left from those on the right as surely as if they were separate countries. We left the interstate for Route 276, then drove a short way to the intersection of old North Carolina 284, which we followed northwest. It soon became a dirt road passing unpainted wooden houses and ramshackle outbuildings. We passed a grocery on the left and came to a fork in the road, took the fork to the right, then continued up and up the muddy, curving road. As the road became more hair-raising, the rain became less violent. We drove 5.8 miles to Cove Creek Gap on the left, the start of our hike, but passed it by on our way to the Cataloochee Ranger Station. From the gap the road descends, coming in a little more than 1½ miles to the new Cataloochee Road where we turned left. Three miles farther on we passed the Cataloochee Primitive Campground on the left and ½ mile beyond that arrived at the ranger station just as the ranger drove in and the sun came out, sudden, brilliant, and strong.

We showed the ranger our itinerary. He suggested we leave the car in the parking area near the ranger station rather than at Cove Creek Gap, then made one change in our last day's hike so that we would come down nearer to it.

"There's a guy going around ripping off cars," he said. "Cove Creek Gap is too isolated. We can keep an eye on it down here. We know his schedule and saturate the area on his days."

From the parking area we now had almost 5 miles uphill to the gap. It was already after 1:00 and we still had 6 miles along the Cataloochee Divide to hike before setting up camp. The ranger issued us our permit and we drove the car to the parking area, gathered up our packs, located loose-lying boots, and, miraculously, got a ride to Cove Creek Gap.

"That's Mount Sterling," our driver said as he rounded a bend just before Cove Creek Gap. We had just told him we would spend our last night at Mount Sterling. He pointed to the left, way off across a valley to a group of pointed, tree-covered mountains. "With the fire tower on it," he said. We looked, but not knowing where we were looking, did not see the tower. He dropped us off, wished us a good trip.

It is 2:30 when we begin our hike. The path climbs gently upward along a weathered split-rail fence dividing the park from the Cataloochee Ranch. The sun streams through the woods on the park side and across the vast meadows of the ranch. Occasional flowering trees burst out in the open spaces against a cloudless sky. We walk along the very top of the ridge, the divide between two mountain areas, and we have constant views to both sides of endless green mountains: peaked, coned, rounded, high but always green. Wild flowers scatter themselves on the forest floor and line the path or lean against the fence. We stop to rest on a log and a salamander runs across it. We open a gate and enter a high meadow just to sit awhile in all that gentle loveliness.

Returning to the path we pass a private home of stone and gray wood (how perfect a hut it would be . . .). A short way on we come to Double Gap at 6.2 miles. To our right the Double Gap Trail enters the Cataloochee Divide, to the left is another gate. We have, by writing beforehand, secured permission to camp on the ranch property, albeit somewhat confused permission. The guidebook told us we could camp there with permission, the writers having apparently obtained permission without mentioning they were writing a guidebook. As a result the ranch people began receiving letters requesting permission to camp, more or less out of the blue. Anyway, their address is: Cataloochee Ranch, Route 1, Box 500, Maggie Valley, North Carolina 28751. (With its rustic, informal atmosphere, it might be a pleasant place to stay in the area. Rates, which include all meals, are reasonable. They outfit wilderness trail rides in the Smokies for the American Forestry Association. For more information, write directly to the ranch.)

We set up camp on top of a hill while a herd of Black Angus mills on the sides and top of the next hill. Their lowing is loud and mournful.

It has been thundering for an hour, although the sky has remained clear. Suddenly, as soon as we get our water boiling, the rain comes. (I somehow believed it would wait until we had eaten and climbed into the tents.) Hard, driving, it lasts long enough to soak everything, then ends in time for us, bedraggled, to eat and go to sleep while it is still light.

Double Gap to Paul's Gap to Spruce
Mountain Fire Tower—10.1 miles, 5 hours

From Double Gap the trail along the divide follows the split-rail fence, then enters the woods as it climbs. Rhododendron line both sides of the trail. A bobcat walks down it toward us, then disappears in an instant into the forest. The trail comes out along the fence again, now edging a vast meadow. The cows have moved up here and a few of them lift their heads to watch us, then go back to their breakfasts. We open a gate and step into the meadow. From here we can see the house we passed yesterday, the ranch, the Maggie Valley, across the valley to further meadows and endless mountains and a Masonic camp perched on the edge of one, looking like some ancient Incan city. We continue south, climbing to Hemphill Bald, at 5,540 feet, the highest point on this trail. We pass through woods full of flowers; deep-red trillium, white trillium, bluet, violets, countless others; turn west and descend along a trail where we find water in a clear and pretty stream, the first water we have passed since yesterday. We stop to fill the bottles.

In a little more than a mile, about 4 miles from Double Gap, the trail heads northwest, now bound on both sides by a thick mass of fringed phacelia; on the uphill side the tiny white flowers continue slightly up the hill, and on the downhill side they slip off the edge and continue downhill. It seems they go on forever, ending only at Paul's Gap, 5.3 miles from Double Gap. At Paul's Gap there is a spur road that comes in from the Blue Ridge Parkway. The trail to the right (east) is the Rough Fork Trail, which goes 8 miles to the New Cataloochee Road. Our trail to Spruce Mountain continues to the left of the Rough Fork Trail. As we head up it we find ourselves suddenly in a tropical jungle, the moist, dark earth of the path under our feet edged by giant rhododendrons forming a tenebrous canopy over the trail, extending back into a forest of twisted, bent, leaning, interwoven, thick rhododendrons; then out of it and through pine woods to the junction of the trail to the Balsam Mountain Road, which goes off to the left about ½ mile before the fire tower at Spruce Mountain. A little gray junco flies up from almost beneath my feet. Looking along the path embankment, I find its nest.

Another 15 minutes and we reach Spruce Mountain (5,590 ft.) with its fire tower and locked-up ranger cabin. Built of handsome, thick spruce logs it would make a good, small hut. We look for water, then discover that, according to the guidebook, we must return to the trail junction and continue some way down on the trail toward the Balsam Mountain Road. None of us feel like going, but we need water. About ¼ mile down the trail (¾ mile from camp) we find a trickle running off the rocks. Using a quart canteen we fill our 2½-gallon jug and carry it back uphill, gather firewood, build a fire, and relax on the porch of the cabin with a little brandy.

In front of the cabin the area is clean, but back behind the tower, where the outhouse had been (knocked over, as of this writing), garbage is strewn everywhere: perhaps by a bear, although little traces of people's untidiness—charred cans and old towels in the fire pit—make us wonder what could be blamed on bears. At dusk we climb the tower from which we have a spectacular 360-degree view of the mountains, although at this hour all the mountains are hardly more than dark and darker shadows in the graying light.

En route to Laurel Gap

Spruce Mountain to Laurel Gap—
about 9 miles, 4 hours

Another day of brilliant sun, clear blue sky—we walk back to the trail junction, down the trail to the Balsam Mountain Road, past our spring of yesterday, down and down, past the waterfall we had heard yesterday when we were looking for water, to the road, and then about 2½ miles along the road—a wonderful dirt road strewn with the white petals of flowering trees; gentle, friendly, beckoning road—to Pin Oak Gap, where we pick up the Balsam Mountain

Trail. We begin to climb, heading northeast in the hot sun, about 2 miles to Ledge Bald at 5,184 feet, only to descend to Beech Gap, a little over 5 miles from Spruce Mountain, then climb again, stopping now and then for lemonade in the hot sun as we make our way to Balsam High Top (5,688 ft.), where we stop, lean back against our packs, and lunch in the hot sun.

We stay an hour there, finally forcing ourselves to continue, but downhill now, arriving, rather suddenly it seems to me, at Laurel Gap Shelter. Tired, we are glad to be here, although the shelter itself, a three-sided stone building with a wire fence and gate on the fourth side, is depressing. Inside are fourteen wire bunks, seven on top, seven on the bottom. Inside, I feel I am in a zoo. The fence, designed to keep bears out, seems to keep mice, birds, and bugs in. And the grounds, particularly around the fire-place, are scattered with litter. It would be nicer to be sleeping in a tent, but it is illegal to pitch tents near a shelter. There is water at the stream, about 200 yards away from the shelter. Two other peo-ple arrive, the first we've seen since we began hiking. They are go-ing the same way we are tomorrow.

There is a luxury of time this afternoon, and I lean, lazily, against the ancient chestnut log that stretches across a little rise above the shelter. The sun is still hot, but now its heat is a reward rather than a burden. Birds flitter in and out of the trees behind me, the grass in front of me is dotted with little clumps of bluet. The fire is going now and I smell the woodsmoke in an evening turning gray. The sun has become a white and indefinable shape.

Laurel Gap to Tricorner Knob—
5.8 miles, about 3 hours

We wake early to rain, and cook in the shelter. At this moment I am glad of the shelter. We wait an hour or so, but the rain never lets up so we finally leave, climbing slightly at first to Balsam Corner where the trail bears left (west), then having an easy walk as the trail levels out, easy except that it is so incredibly wet. My pack, which seemed light at first, quickly feels too heavy. Soon after leaving the shelter we come across a spring and fill the water bottles, and the pack becomes still heavier. The trail is one long puddle after another, either to be straddled or to be avoided by climbing up the side in the wet grass or flowers, which I am reluctant to do; yet the strain of straddling sometimes forces me up into a slightly more comfortable position. The flowers close up or turn their backs to the rain. Huge fallen trees bare their massive roots, others lie in every direction, blow-downs caused by the great winds that often sweep across this ridge. To the left, flowering trees glow white through the gray morning. A little over a mile brings us to the junction of the Gunter Fork Trail to Walnut Bottom and Big Creek.

The rain does not abate. My boots soon have puddles in them, the rain soaks through my poncho (which has, until now, proven utterly trustworthy), and the parka and shirt I wear underneath it are quickly wet. The wind, while luckily not severe, nevertheless blows across the ridge without a stop and I feel cold. The pack gets heavier. I long to sit—just for a little while, to be rid of the pack—just for a little while.

Two people come toward us and announce we are 500 yards from the shelter. It seems to me a very long 500 yards until, suddenly, it is there. We smell a wood fire and enter the Tricorner Knob Shelter (5,960 ft.). It is filled with people, most of them bundled in sleeping bags, all of them avoiding going outside. Someone by the fire offers us hot onion soup. I am so grateful. We take off most of our wet clothes, although there is hardly anyplace left to hang them. Slowly we begin to dry out and warm up. The people at the fire move away so we can get close to it. My jeans are wet where the rain chaps don't cover, and four hours later I still feel chilled. New people come in, then six people leave, and the shelter is uncrowded and comfortable for a while. Four more people arrive, filling the shelter to capacity. The rain continues. My sleeping bag feels damp and I begin to dread tomorrow if no sun comes to dry us out.

Tricorner Knob is on the Appalachian Trail, and there are a

Tricorner Knob Shelter

few through-hikers on their way from Georgia to Maine at the shelter. Two of them, a couple nestled in the corner, are packing a guitar. Four people in their fifties or so are doing the Appalachian Trail in sections—two weeks of it each year.

Tricorner Knob to Cosby Knob—
7.6 miles, 3½ hours

The sky is tentative. Clouds; clouds dispersing; blue; clouds; mist; a ray of bright sun. We start out in the wrong direction, headed toward Peck's Corner, downhill. After 2 miles we meet two men who tell us we are wrong. It was my fault and I am furious at the extra 4 miles it caused with the 2 we now have to go, uphill at that, but there is nothing to do but to do it. Back at Tricorner Knob we continue uphill, but gently, around Mount Guyot (at 6,621 feet, the second-highest peak in the Smokies). There is an unmaintained and fairly obscure trail to the top of Mount Guyot going off our trail to the right (south). We ignore it, walking through mist-shrouded trees, spruce and fir reaching up ghostly, dark in the now gray sky.

I am cold, wearing only a T-shirt, but everything else is still too wet to put on. The air remains, since the rain, too damp to dry things. We continue level, to a gap (6,180 ft.) between Guyot and Old Black (6,356 ft.) where the sun comes out. There is a mar-velous open view of mountains and meadows to the east from here, and we luxuriate in it and the sun's heat. Suddenly a mist begins rolling down the path from Guyot, through the forest, out of the forest, rolling steadily toward us, expanding as it reaches the gap, enveloping us as we stand, awed, watching the progress of this live and growing thing, until it sends us on. We walk up Old Black, then down almost the entire way to Cosby Knob at 4,800 ft.

A little over a mile from Old Black the trail comes to Inadu Knob and the junction of the Maddron Bald Trail to the left (west and northeast). We remain on the Appalachian Trail, which turns to the right (east) and follows the ridge line. It is the first path we've been on with large boulders and rocky outcroppings. Some-times it passes through soft grass with views to the right (south), then through a rhododendron jungle, all the while the sun and mist still playing leapfrog. A gentle rain falls now and then. We walk over small rocks on a path that becomes a shallow creek with the rain that has already fallen. At Camel Gap, a little more than 2 miles from Inadu Knob, we pass the junction of the Yellow Creek Trail to Walnut Bottom on the right (south), while the Appalachian Trail begins to climb, gently but consistently, through a world of grass and wild flowers, now totally mist-shrouded.

We arrive at the shelter to find the two men who had told us we were wrong and two other people from Tricorner Knob who couldn't imagine how it had taken us so long to get there and two through-hikers who talked only to each other. (The time, 3½ hours, at the head of this section is figured *without* my diversion.) The twelve-man shelter and area around it are clean. It has an atmosphere we found neither at Laurel Gap nor at Tricorner Knob and we are glad to be here.

We cook and eat and try to sleep, although after a mouse runs across the rafter over my bunk as I get into my sleeping bag, I spend most of the night listening for his return. I hear him chewing a good deal. An owl hoots—eerie, mournful—on his nightly rounds. Rain falls again, splattering on the tin roof.

There are two reasons for selecting lower bunks in the Smokies' shelters, even if they make you feel (as they do me) claustrophobic —one is that the mice seem to prefer the higher rafters, the other is that sometimes the roof leaks.

Cosby Knob to Mount Sterling— 10½ miles, about 6 hours

Morning dawns sunny and warm. Just that prepares me for anything. We are able to eat outside, pack up, and leave early, starting off downhill. In slightly less than a mile we come to Low Gap where our route, the Low Gap Trail, turns right (east) for the 2.3-mile hike to Walnut Bottom. The trail to the left (northwest) to Cosby Campground and the Appalachian Trail continues straight ahead (north) to Mount Cammerer and Davenport Gap. We continue descending through woods. Water runs everywhere in little creeks and falls until we reach Big Creek, where a broad watercourse tumbles over rounded rocks, clear and inviting. Eventually we come to a path leading down to it and get our fill of water for washing and drinking. We climb back up to the trail and continue on to Walnut Bottom where the trail we must now follow, the Swallow Fork Trail, is not marked for anyone coming from this direction. We turn left, walk up the dirt road a short way to a bridge where there is a sign. The trail goes off to the left (southeast), immediately ascends past a horse trough (spring), and continues up for almost 4 miles before coming to Pretty Hollow Gap, then climbs another 1½ miles to Mount Sterling. There is water everywhere along the first part of this route. Near its start, the path climbs quickly above Big Creek, then crosses it at a wide and fairly deep point. There is no bridge. The current is fast and strong. We take off our boots, socks, and jeans and wade across. The water is icy, the flat rocks underfoot slippery. (See pp. 23–24 for the *proper* way to cross a stream.)

Feeling quite triumphant we dress and continue up the path, only to come to another crossing. The water is less deep, so we take off only shoes and socks. I find a sturdy walking stick someone has abandoned—obviously thinking he was through with stream crossings. It helps enormously and I hold on to it for the third crossing, still farther up. For the third one we do not bother to remove shoes. Shortly past the third crossing, about 2 miles from Walnut Bottom, we come to a large white quartz boulder. Less than ¼ mile beyond the boulder we cross a small stream where one finds the last water on the trail in a falls tumbling over mossy rocks, just where the trail bends.

We stop for lunch, fill our water bottles, and continue up on a path through a mass of rhododendron, another tropical jungle. Half a mile from the falls and climbing all the time, the trail turns sharply to the right. The sun now is very hot. In just under a mile from the sharp turn we reach Pretty Hollow Gap, where we encounter a troop of girl scouts on their way up to Mount Sterling, getting in shape for a summer trip to Wyoming.

Pretty Hollow Gap is the junction of the trail to Laurel Gap to the right (southwest), the Pretty Hollow Gap Trail straight ahead, leading to the Cataloochee Road, and the Mount Sterling Ridge Trail (ours), which turns left and follows the Mount Sterling Ridge, a lovely walk with many good views early in the season. (Later on the trees block much of it.)

It is about 1 mile from the junction to the fire tower on Mount Sterling (5,842 ft.). By the time we reach it there are already many campers settled in. This is a Saturday night at a campsite about 2½ miles from a road (old North Carolina 284 to the east). We try to ignore them, but it does feel a bit like being on a popular beach. The fire tower here offers wonderful views in all directions, but the locked-up ranger's cabin somehow lacks the charm of the one on Balsam Mountain (a subjective view, I'm sure). The guidebook says there is no water here, but in fact there is a small trickle of a spring 100 yards below the tower.

We pitch our tents facing the sunrise—if only there is a sunrise.

Mount Sterling to Cataloochee Ranger Station via Long Bunk and Little Cataloochee—about 12 miles, about 6 hours

It rains during the night. I find it nice to hear on the tent. There is no wind. It is not raining by morning, although thunder rumbles and the sky is gray; streaks of gray and lighter gray. We make breakfast and begin to pack up just in time to run back into the tents when the rain breaks. During a lull we strike the tents and begin our walk down. It begins to rain again as we make our way past the horse hitching posts to the junction of the Mount Sterling Ridge and Mount Sterling Gap trails, turn to the left, and follow the Mount Sterling Gap Trail as it winds down about 2 miles along a rocky, mossy ledge, then turn off to the right (southeast) to Long Bunk (also called Pig Pen) where, contrary to the guidebook, there is a sign. Some time back it had stopped raining but now begins again—a great deluge.

The thick, rich mud of the trail slows us; it oozes around our boots, sucks them in as we make our way, separately wrapped in mud and rain, through the gleaming, dark forest. A grouse flies up from her nest out of the wet silence. The sudden, violent flapping of wings startles us. She crosses to the other side of the trail and, from a fallen log, continues flapping her wings and hissing, her face as violent as her sounds. We hurry past the nest and the forest is quiet again, the ancient, moss-covered logs soaking up yet another century of rain.

The trail descends most of the way, once or twice climbing a little along the side of a hill, finally widening into an old, and now unused, road which the former inhabitants of these hills used. We find the remains of buildings: a pig shelter, barns, cabins. The sun begins to play with the rain, finally chasing the rain away. We sit awhile on a wet log in the sun, then continue on, coming to a well-kept cemetery with fresh flowers, all the stones marking graves of the Hannah clan. Shortly afterward, a little more than 5 miles from Mount Sterling, we come to the end of Long Bunk and the beginning of the Little Cataloochee Trail, which we will follow for the next 4 miles. We pass another house (built 1862) of the Hannah clan and come, about ½ mile beyond it, to a bridge over the Little Cataloochee Creek. The sun is fully out now, and we drape all our wet things over the sides of the bridge, then sit down on the warm wood planks for lunch. The water rushes along beneath us, the sun streams into us—a perfect spot.

Continuing on we come to the Little Cataloochee Baptist Church, still maintained by local families, its plain white structure clean and simple in the noon sun. The trail, a jeep road for a while, climbs, descends, then, narrowed again, begins the steepest climb of our entire route, gaining 900 feet in a mile as it ascends a wooded, wild-flowered hill to Davidson Gap (3,820 ft.). From the gap it descends, steeply at first, following Coggins Branch, which has spilled over, and runs haphazardly down the trail and off into the woods again. The trail is, once more, quite wet. Nearing its end it follows an old road and comes finally to Palmer Creek with its wide, beautiful, clear water rushing around boulders, through

rapids, over falls. We turn left (southeast), follow the Palmer Creek
Trail 0.7 mile to the New Cataloochee Road and the end of our trip,
save for the walk of about 2 miles down the paved road to the
ranger station and the car. There is almost no traffic on this sunny
afternoon. We walk along the split-rail fence. Behind it there are
endless green fields dotted with blue flowers and, over everything,
a great peace.

ΛΛ\

For all the talk about crowds here, we never saw them except at
Mount Sterling on a Saturday night. I would certainly make any future trips in the spring and try not to include a Saturday night.
While we had the trails in Cataloochee to ourselves, the Appalachian
Trail was hardly overburdened, since the shelter regulations to
some extent limit the numbers of hikers on the trail. The hiking is
easy and relaxed, and this could be a good place for an experienced
hiker to make a first backpacking trip. But not without superb
raingear. The rain here can turn the most gentle path into an ordeal.

This is an area where changes are imminent. About 76 percent
of the park will become a wilderness area as soon as Congress acts
on the proposals currently before it. This can happen any time.
Once Congress acts, the shelters are scheduled to be removed. This
is being done not because they have no place in wilderness areas
(the Park Service does not think of them as permanent since they
have no foundations) but because, in spite of permits issued according to shelter capacity, there are still great numbers of people
without permits camping in the shelter areas. A more effective way
of getting rid of illegal campers, during the busy season, might be
to institute a caretaker system, which I discuss in Part Three of this
book.

Mount Le Conte Lodge is also scheduled to be closed. The
current concessioner's contract runs to December 31, 1977. But

there has been a great outpouring of objections to its closing. Nevertheless, the size of the lodge, the type of soil on which it stands and over which horses must carry supplies to it, the kind of climate—much rain and low temperatures—in which it exists, cause maintainance, ecological, and health problems. They are being worked on, and if they can be solved, the Park Service would keep it open.

7 White Mountain National Forest, New Hampshire—*From Franconia Notch to Carter Notch*

It seems an old land, gentle and removed from time. White clapboard villages nestle in narrow valleys over which ancient mountains stand eternal, temperate guard. Crystal streams lace a tranquil countryside where cows graze in the pastures as they did 200 years ago—a rural world of silence and peace.

Suddenly the gentleness explodes into a maze of steep, rocky trails leading forever up through dense forests of beech, birch, maple, spruce, and fir; up the routes of dried-up streams that one time plunged in violent falls as do others now, rushing turbulent, white and tameless, relentlessly down. The mountains, so green from the valley, become bare, mist-shrouded, wild with the wildness of great, high mountains, lost to the gentle removes of time; fierce, cold, and glorious.

New Hampshire is a tourist state. By American standards it is one of venerable age. Settled in 1623, it set up a provisional, revolutionary government six months before the rest of the colonies. Tourists come to witness its history, to indulge in its resorts—both moun-

One steep trail

tain and seaside—to gaze upon its scenic attractions and the colors of its autumn. For those who leave the roads behind it offers some of the most challenging and varied hiking in the country.

A LITTLE NATURAL HISTORY

The most spectacular ranges of this mountainous state are found in the White Mountains. Part of the Appalachian system, they stretch a few miles from the Connecticut River in the west across the north-central part of the state and on into western Maine. A good part of them, both in New Hampshire and in Maine, are contained in White Mountain National Forest. The 683,637 acres of forest land in New Hampshire include the Presidential Range with the highest peaks in the White Mountains. The highest is the 6,288-foot Mount Washington. It is also the highest in the Northeast.

The Presidentials lie between the Franconia Range (separated by Crawford Notch) and the Carter-Moriah Range (separated by Pinkham Notch). The hike that follows begins in the Franconia Range, traverses the Presidentials, and ends in the Carter-Moriah Range, a distance of about 53 miles. *Notch* is the local name for pass.

Throughout these mountains you will see game birds in plenty, but relatively few animals, made shy by so many years of civilization and hunters. But they are there—deer, bears, snowshoe hare, raccoons, fox. Rabbits and squirrels are common and there has been recent talk of coyote, or coyotelike animals, as well.

White Mountain National Forest contains two wilderness areas. The Great Gulf Wilderness, established in 1959, includes 5,552 acres on the north side of Mount Washington, while the 20,380 acres of the Presidential Range–Dry River Wilderness, which came into existence in January 1975, spread southward from Mount Washington, beginning shortly below the Tuckerman Crossover.

There are shelters in the Presidential Range–Dry River Wilderness, but these will be removed, and not replaced, as they decay. Those in the Great Gulf have been removed. Regulations for camping in these areas are available from: Forest Service Headquarters, P.O. Box 638, Laconia, New Hampshire 03246.

The Forest Service people in the White Mountains have been conscientious in reaching out to the public through outdoor magazines, backpacking shops, mailing lists, etc., in their attempt to develop a forest-wide management policy. The public has, more or less, been involved with the White Mountains since 1605, when Mount Washington was first seen from the sea. It was first climbed

Ice-covered trees in August at the top of Ammonoosuc Ravine

in 1642, nineteen years after New Hampshire was settled and a remarkably early date in the history of mountaineering. By the nineteenth century, when the Romance of the Wilderness was at its height, vacationers from the cities thronged to the White Mountains. It was an active time in mountaineering in America as well as in the Alps, in trail building, and in inclinations toward wilderness preservation. The Appalachian Mountain Club (AMC), the first mountaineering club in America, was founded in 1876. From the beginning it has been fully involved in the development and preservation of these mountains, although paths were being carved out of the Whites by farmers, hunters, and hotel keepers long before the AMC appeared. Many of the early trails are still in use. The first section of the Crawford Path (see p. 225), for instance, was cut in 1819. By 1888 the AMC had constructed its first hut, the Madison Hut (since destroyed by fire and rebuilt in 1941). Meanwhile, the railroad penetrated deep into remote valleys and large, rambling, comfortable mountain hotels flourished.

CIVILIZED AMENITIES

Today the AMC's hut system includes eight rustic and simple huts plus Pinkham Notch Camp, all situated about a good, long day's hike apart. All of them can be reached from a variety of directions, some of which provide easy, comfortable hikes. The routes between huts, however, are not easy, or if the route is, the weather may well not be. The level, exposed ridge followed by the Crawford Path from the Mizpah Springs Hut to the Lakes of the Clouds Hut below Mount Washington enjoys some of the worst weather in the world.

The huts are open to the public but reservations are essential. For any or all of the huts, write or call: Huts Manager, Pinkham Notch Camp, Gorham, New Hampshire 03581; (603) 466-2727. While there are a few variations in opening and closing dates, the huts are, in general, open for the summer season from mid-June to Labor Day. Specifics are available from Pinkham Notch. As of this writing the cost is $14.50 per person, which includes a bunk with mattress and blankets, dinner, breakfast, and a trail lunch. (It costs $1.00 more at Pinkham Notch Camp, which is large, bustling, and accessible by car, but you get sheets.) Meals are served family-style at 7:00 A.M. and 6:00 P.M.

If you are just passing by one of the huts, but not staying, you can stop in for hot chocolate anytime during the day. You need not stay in huts to follow this route, since campgrounds and shelters along the way require only slight deviations from these specific trails. There is no camping around the huts except at the Mizpah-Nauman Campsite (see p. 226), and no camping above timberline because of the fragile nature of the vegetation.

If you are following the hike described and have one car at your disposal, you will have a hitch of over an hour to get back to it at the end of the hike. If you are traveling by bus you still have short hitches at the beginning and end. It is about 4½ miles south on Routes 18 and 3 from Franconia to the start of the trail in Franconia Notch. At the finish, from the end of 19-Mile Brook Trail, it is a little more than 2 miles south on Route 16 to Pinkham Notch Camp where you can catch a bus to Boston, the main connecting point for anyone from out of the region. Continental Trailways and Vermont Transit provide the bulk of the bus service, which includes transportation to Franconia, Pinkham Notch, and most of the other villages in the area. If it is impossible to arrive at Franconia on the same day you plan to begin your hike, you will find a variety of accommodations, including a few lovely old inns. For information, write: Franconia–Sugar Hill–Easton Chamber of Commerce, Franconia, New Hampshire 03580. The Lafayette Campground is directly across the road (Route 3) in Franconia Notch from the start of this hike. You may camp there (fee) or leave your car. The campground is about 2 miles south of the Cannon Mountain Aerial Tramway and a 1⅓-mile hike from the AMC hut at Lonesome Lake to the west, the only AMC hut not included in the route that follows.

SPECIAL REGULATIONS

Free wilderness permits are required for camping in both wilderness areas. The Great Gulf Wilderness requires permits for *day* use as well as overnight use. Day-use permits may be obtained from any ranger station or at Pinkham Notch Camp. Overnight permits *must* be obtained from the Androscoggin Ranger Station, Gorham, New Hampshire 03581. Overnight use in the Great Gulf is limited, but you may reserve space here up to a month in advance. For the Presidential Range–Dry River Wilderness, permits may be obtained from any ranger station, the Forest Supervisor's Office, the **AMC**, Crawford Notch State Park, Mount Washington State Park, or either of the two new information stations on I-93. Permits may be obtained by mail from the ranger stations or supervisor's office. Permits are also required for camping in Tuckerman and Huntington ravines. Neither locale is in a wilderness area, but both are heavily used and subject to overnight limits. These permits, which cost $1.50, are on a first come, first served basis. Purchase them at Pinkham Notch Camp.

Everywhere else in White Mountain National Forest fire permits are required for any campers who plan to build a fire. Even if you expect to use your stove all the time, a fire permit is a good idea in case the stove breaks, or you run out of fuel, or the idea of a campfire suddenly seems irresistible. Throughout the forest neither campfires nor camping is allowed above timberline. A restricted-use area program is in effect and regulations vary from area to area. At some campsites there are nominal fees. Check out all current regulations before you start off on your hike, either with any of the ranger stations listed on pp. 218–19 or at one of the two new information stations on I-93. The Campton exit station is just south of the forest, and the Lincoln exit station is located at about mid-forest. Fire permits are available by writing, phoning, or stopping at one of the ranger stations or stopping at one of the information stations.

BOOKS AND MAPS

White Mountain Guide, published by the Appalachian Mountain Club. Cloth, $9.00. Small enough to fit in your pack, but cloth-bound and sturdy, it is absolutely indispensable for anyone hiking in the White Mountains. It contains all the necessary maps.

AMC Guide to Mount Washington and the Presidential Range, Howard Goff and the Editors of the *AMC White Mountain Guide,* introduction by Mary Minor Smith; published by the Appalachian Mountain Club. Paperback, $3.95. A compact guide and reference, map included, for anyone planning to hike only in the Presidentials.

Mountain Flowers of New England, Stuart K. Harris, Frederick Steele, Miriam Underhill; published by the Appalachian Mountain Club. Paperback, $6.50.

Don't Die on the Mountain, Dan Allen, published by the Appalachian Mountain Club. Paperback, $1.00. A small and helpful guide to the objective and subjective dangers of hiking in the White Mountains.

By far the best maps are those that come with the *AMC White Mountain Guide*. These maps may also be purchased singly. Latex maps of Mount Washington and of the Franconia region cost $1.00 each; paper maps of Mount Washington, the Franconia region, Carter-Mahoosuc, and Chocorua-Waterville cost 50¢ each. They, and the above books, are available from: AMC Book Sale, 5 Joy Street, Boston, Massachusetts 02108.

There is no single USGS topo map for the entire region, but you could put together a series of them: 15-minute "Mt. Washington," 15-minute "Crawford Notch," 7.5-minute "Franconia," 7.5-minute "South Twin," and 7.5-minute "Carter Dome."

FOREST SERVICE RANGER OFFICES

Ammonoosuc Ranger District
Box 239 (Trudeau Road)
Bethlehem, New Hampshire 03754

Androscoggin Ranger District
Glen Road
Gorham, New Hampshire 03581

Pemigewasset Ranger District
127 Highland Street
Plymouth, New Hampshire 03264

Saco Ranger District
Kancamagus Highway (P.O. Box 274)
Gorham, New Hampshire 03581

The address for forest headquarters is:
Forest Supervisor
White Mountain National Forest
P.O. Box 638
Laconia, New Hampshire 03246
(603) 524–6450

The ranger station in Maine is:
Evans Notch Ranger District
Bridge Street
Bethel, Maine 04217

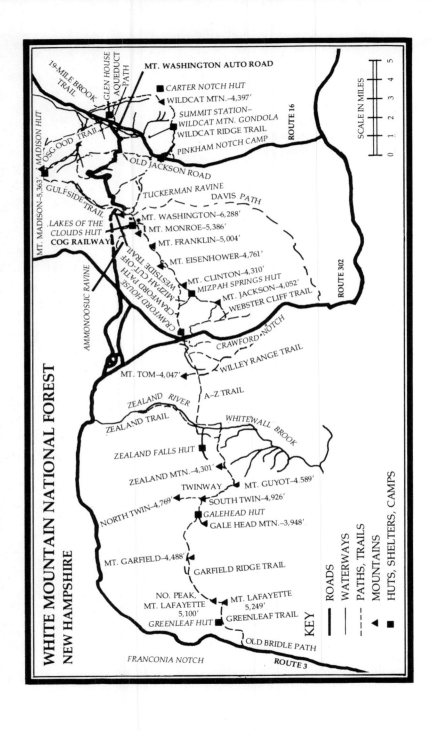

WHITE MOUNTAIN NATIONAL FOREST
NEW HAMPSHIRE

MT. WASHINGTON AUTO ROAD

19-MILE BROOK TRAIL
GLEN HOUSE
AQUEDUCT PATH
CARTER NOTCH HUT
WILDCAT MTN.–4,397'
SUMMIT STATION–
WILDCAT MTN. GONDOLA
WILDCAT RIDGE TRAIL
PINKHAM NOTCH CAMP
ROUTE 16

MADISON HUT
OSGOOD TRAIL
OLD JACKSON ROAD

MT. MADISON–5,363'
GULFSIDE TRAIL
TUCKERMAN RAVINE
DAVIS PATH

LAKES OF THE
CLOUDS HUT
COG RAILWAY
MT. WASHINGTON–6,288'
MT. MONROE–5,386'
MT. FRANKLIN–5,004'

MT. EISENHOWER–4,761'

WESTSIDE TRAIL
MIZPAH CUT-OFF
MT. CLINTON–4,310'
MIZPAH SPRINGS HUT
MT. JACKSON–4,052'
WEBSTER CLIFF TRAIL

AMMONOOSUC RAVINE
CRAWFORD HOUSE
CRAWFORD PATH
CRAWFORD NOTCH

WILLEY RANGE TRAIL

ROUTE 302

MT. TOM–4,047'
A–Z TRAIL

ZEALAND RIVER
ZEALAND TRAIL
WHITEWALL BROOK

ZEALAND FALLS HUT
ZEALAND MTN.–4,301'
TWINWAY
MT. GUYOT–4,589'
SOUTH TWIN–4,926'
NORTH TWIN–4,769'
GALEHEAD HUT
GALE HEAD MTN.–3,948'

MT. GARFIELD–4,488'
GARFIELD RIDGE TRAIL

NO. PEAK,
MT. LAFAYETTE
5,100'
MT. LAFAYETTE
5,249'
GREENLEAF HUT
GREENLEAF TRAIL
OLD BRIDLE PATH
FRANCONIA NOTCH
ROUTE 3

SCALE IN MILES
0 1 2 3 4 5

KEY
ROADS
WATERWAYS
PATHS, TRAILS
MOUNTAINS
HUTS, SHELTERS, CAMPS

Lafayette Place to Greenleaf Hut—
2½ miles, about 2½ hours

It is already midafternoon in early September when I leave Lafayette Place for the uphill hike to Greenleaf Hut. Crossing the road from the campground, I follow the path northeast into the woods. Almost immediately it begins to climb, but moderately as it heads southeast, then turns north, making its way along the edge of the ridge. There are spectacular views of Mount Lincoln and the whole Franconia Ridge including Mount Lafayette, a part of tomorrow's route, to the north of Mount Lincoln. Not far beyond these views the path enters a stand of stunted spruce and continues level a short ways. The views now are to the west, across Franconia Notch to Cannon Mountain. Now the trail becomes steep and rocky, and in the hot, late afternoon of my first day in the White Mountains, I feel the climb. From this steepest part it is not much farther to the hut at 4,200 feet, about 2,400 feet above the road. The path finally reaches the junction of the Greenleaf Trail, a slightly shorter, steeper, and less scenic route from the road to the hut and then, just above tree line, the little hut itself. Just in time for dinner at 6:00, I deposit my pack in the bunkroom, wash up, and join the others at one of the long tables in the hut's main room. I am tired and glad to be here.

Greenleaf Hut to Galehead Hut—
8 miles, about 6½ hours

I leave the hut after a hearty breakfast, head downhill on the Greenleaf Trail in front of the hut, pass Eagle Lake, and begin the ascent of Mount Lafayette (5,249 ft.), over 1,000 feet in slightly more than a mile. The sun was out when I left the hut, but as I begin to climb up the stony path a mist rolls in and all the world, except for the path and a small bit of mountain before me, is cut out. The way continues east up the mountain until about ¼ mile below the summit when it bears north. In thick, damp fog I reach the windswept top, and without being able to see more than the glistening rock at my feet, feel exuberant at being high up in this open, treeless world. I would like to spend some time up here, but the wind and damp make it cold, not a place to dawdle, and throwing on my poncho I turn left (north) onto the Garfield Ridge Trail. (To the south the Franconia Ridge Trail leads to the Liberty Spring Shelter and the Flume and back down to Route 3 to the west, or south to the Kancamagus Highway northeast of Lincoln.) The Garfield Ridge Trail descends slightly to the north peak of Lafayette Mountain (5,100 ft.). A short way on, the Skookumchuck Trail branches off to the left, heading to Route 3. I pass it, head northeast, descend to timberline, and remain on the ridge, passing south of Garfield Pond where a trail to the left goes to Garfield Pond Shelter (AMC) north of the pond. My path then begins to climb again, bearing right (east) shortly before the summit of Mount Garfield (4,488 ft.). (The trail to the left is the Garfield Trail back down to Route 3.)

From here I begin a steep descent down a rocky path, come to a brook, continue on, past the junction with the Franconia Brook Trail to the right. The trail goes continually up and down, arriving, about 2½ miles from Mount Garfield, at the junction with the Gale River Trail down to Route 3 on the left (north). As I continue on, the hut comes into occasional view, but it always seems a long way off, until, finally, I begin the last climb up to it at 3,948 feet. I am glad to drop my pack on the hut's porch and settle down by the window with a cup of hot chocolate. Glad? It is fantastic luxury! After a while I carry my pack in, settle myself in the bunkroom, and just have time to wash before dinner.

Galehead Hut to Zealand Falls Hut—
8 miles, about 6 hours

This morning is brilliant and cool. I leave immediately after breakfast, descending a short ways from the hut, then begin the climb on the Twinway to the top—or almost to the top—the path remains

50 feet below the 4,926-foot summit of South Twin. (A path to the left, the North Twin Spur, goes over the summit.) The wind is cold on South Twin, but the sun and high, open view inviting, so I settle back against the rocks for some tea. A school group comes up from the way I am headed and stops to rest before continuing on over North Twin. On my way again, I turn to the right (south) and descend over white rocks to a col between South Twin and Mount Guyot. A family of partridge sit in the path, idly move to the edge of it as I pass. I begin the climb up Mount Guyot (4,589 ft.), passing the junction with the Bondcliff Trail to the right (south), and continuing toward the left, climb the last 200 yards to the northwest peak of Mount Guyot, then descend the long ridge through lovely birch forest before climbing up again to Zealand Mountain. I bear right onto Zealand Ridge, which descends to the left of Zeacliff

On top of South Twin

Pond, and pass the junction of the Zeacliff Trail (to the right) where I turn left, continue down the ridge, cross Whitewall Brook, pass the junction (to the left) of the Lend-a-Hand Trail where I turn right, and come, soon after the junction, to Zealand Falls Hut.

Zealand Falls Hut to Crawford House—
5 miles, about 4 hours

The steep, rocky path from the hut leads down for about ¼ mile through woods, past Zealand Falls. I make a little detour to the right for a view of the falls, then, back on the path, continue steeply down a short ways to the junction of the Zealand Trail, which I follow to the left for about another ¼ mile to the junction of the A–Z Trail, which I now follow to the right. The trail crosses a number of small streams, then climbs easily for about 2 miles, after which it climbs more steeply up to the junction of the Willey Range Trail to the right (down to Route 302 in Crawford Notch). A little past the junction a trail to the left goes off to Mount Tom (4,047 ft.). Now a descent over a wide, stony, persistent path begins. Half a mile beyond the Mount Tom junction my path crosses a stream and proceeds another ½ mile to the junction of the Mount Avalon Trail, passes the Mount Willard Trail, crosses a footbridge, and comes to the wide, green lawns of Crawford House, a sprawling, white hotel built in the late 1850s.*

Highway 302 runs through Crawford Notch, past a small lake, a railroad station that has become a coffee shop without trains, a gas station, and on through the notch itself. The old hotel sits there in faded grandeur. Inside, the lobby is big and empty. The chairs wait for guests who will arrive next week to see the leaves. Bowls of plastic flowers adorn the tables. One lamp is lit and the only sound is the ticking of the clock. On one wall hangs a portrait of a man who spent 92 consecutive seasons as a guest at Crawford

---

* Since this trip Crawford House has unfortunately been dismantled. One must now walk the additional 2½ miles directly to Mizpah Springs Hut, described in the following hike.

House. I leave my pack in my room, shower, and head for the old railroad station and a beer. It's a very good beer.

Crawford House to Mizpah Springs Hut—
2½ miles, 2 hours; Mizpah Springs Hut to
Mount Jackson and back—3½ miles,
about 2 hours

Mists rise off the mountains on both sides of the notch and in places the early sun breaks through the clouds. Spots of red and gold from the first changed trees stand out from the mass of green that covers the mountains. I wait for the dining room to open for breakfast, eat and afterward cross the road to begin my hike up to the hut on the Crawford Path. It is a steady uphill through spruce and balsam woods along the south bank of Gibbs Brook, which I can hear but cannot see. After 1¾ miles the Mizpah Cut-off branches off the Crawford Path to the right (east), while the Crawford Path continues its way up to Mount Clinton. (It is this section, Crawford to Mount Clinton, mentioned earlier.) I take the cut-off, which continues the climb a short way, then levels off and descends the last few feet to the hut where it joins the Webster Cliff Trail. The hut sits at the junction of the Webster Cliff, Mizpah Cut-off, and Mount Clinton trails.

Mizpah Springs Hut (3,800 ft.) is the newest (1965) and largest of the AMC huts. It is a handsome, comfortable hut set in a sunny open space. I have a lovely lunch outside before starting out on an excursion to Mount Jackson via the Webster Cliff Trail, an easy hike. The path climbs gradually at first, then remains mostly level as it heads southeast and south, winding through woods. The path is muddy but planks have been laid across much of the mud. Passing through scrub and up a little rock, the trail comes, 1¾ miles from the hut, to the top of Mount Jackson. From the hut it had looked so far away. Now, from the wonderful, exposed, rocky top I can see the hut to the north and beyond it Mount Washington and all the southern peaks of the Presidentials. It is a place to dally and I do. On the way back just below the summit I notice the trail to my right (east) leading to the Nauman Shelters, one of the few places near a hut where one may camp. (Check with Pinkham Notch Camp regarding fee—as of this writing $1.00 per person.)

Mizpah Springs Hut to Lakes of the Clouds
Hut—4⅔ miles, about 3 hours

Rain began during dinner, kept on and off all night. Morning dawns gray, misty, damp, cold. High winds are reported on the ridge. I have been so looking forward to this long, exposed walk along the ridge and am disappointed to find such weather. I wonder whether Mount Washington will be possible. A few people leave the hut, headed for Lakes of the Clouds. I, too, finally manage to get myself out into the weather and up the Mount Clinton path, over the 4,310-foot Mount Clinton where the path rejoins the Crawford Path. Almost immediately upon leaving the hut I am greeted by the bright yellow warning sign: STOP. THE AREA AHEAD HAS THE WORST WEATHER IN AMERICA. MANY HAVE DIED THERE FROM EXPOSURE, EVEN IN SUMMER. TURN BACK NOW IF THE WEATHER IS BAD. Life, for a coward, is full of so many decisions. Did this, in fact, constitute bad weather? I decide to go on—since I have adequate gear, compass, map, and no reluctance to not climb Mount Washington once I get to the hut if the weather doesn't get better.

The entire way from Mount Clinton to Mount Washington is above tree line, and as soon as I enter the Crawford Path I feel the full force of the fierce and cold wind. It takes great energy to walk through it. I am, one moment, excited at being so exposed, exhilarated by the weather and the sheer damp, powerful emptiness of the world, and the next moment exhausted by it. I hardly care that I have no views, so wild and all-enveloping is this walk which, once past Mount Clinton, remains generally level as it traverses these scrub-scattered heights. Then, suddenly, to the west, the fog lifts in one small stripe and far below me are green hills and bright sun. The fog settles in again. The stripe suddenly appears some-where else, farther on, is closed over, and does not reappear.

The trail is marked by cairns and, in good weather, gives fan-tastic views in every direction as it winds about on top of the ridge. About a mile past Mount Clinton the Mount Eisenhower Loop branches off to the left (west) to cross over the top of 4,761-foot Mount Eisenhower before rejoining the main Crawford Path about ½ mile farther on. This is an easy and pleasant climb in good weather. In this weather I remain on the main path, which continues to the right on the east side of the mountain, coming to a col be-tween Mounts Eisenhower and Franklin where the path passes Red Pond (stagnant). A short way beyond the point at which the Mount Eisenhower Loop reenters the main trail, the Edmands Path leading down to the Mount Clinton Road joins it from the left (west), while the Mount Eisenhower Trail, leading down to a shelter and ulti-mately to Route 302, joins it on the right. Meanwhile, the Crawford Path ascends to Mount Franklin and comes to the Mount Monroe

Interior, Lakes of the Clouds Hut

Loop, which branches off to the left to climb the 5,386-foot, double-peaked Mount Monroe before rejoining the main path near the Lakes of the Clouds Hut. This loop offers another easy ascent in good weather. The trail entering the Crawford Path from the right and continuing on to Mount Monroe is the Dry River Trail, which leads on the right down to a shelter and beyond to a junction with the Mount Eisenhower Trail.

Exactly at the moment the cold seems unbearable, the hut miraculously appears. An Irish setter bounds down the hill toward it and in, as I open the door. The hut is jammed with a Saturday crowd waiting for the weather to change. It is so short a way from here to the top. Shivering, I drink endless cups of hot chocolate, then, 2 hours later, just to get away from the crowds, head out into a bleak, bare landscape—rock and fog marked by cairns stretching across the top of the world like some Tibetan prayer symbols—the Tuckerman Crossover—to the top of the Tuckerman Ravine Headwall. From here rocks lead down the long, very steep, often slippery descent to the Hermit Lake Shelters and on to Pinkham Notch.

Lakes of the Clouds Hut to Madison Hut—
7⅓ miles, about 5 hours

The weather is better in the morning and I start out once again on the Crawford Path, cross the outlet of the larger Lake of the Clouds. The trail to the left, the Ammonoosuc Ravine, provides a sheltered way down from the ridge in bad weather. In spite of a rocky start at the top it is the easiest route down, leading through the ravine to Base Road and the Marshfield Station of the Cog Railway up Mount Washington. (Built in 1869, the charming old train makes the 3-mile trip to the summit in about an hour.) Just past the smaller lake the Camel Trail to Boott Spur and the Tuckerman Crossover branch off to the right. The Boott Spur Trail ends up at Pinkham Notch. The Crawford Path climbs gradually, is joined after about ½ mile by the Davis Path (which connects with the Boott Spur).

A short way on, the Westside Trail branches off to the left, bound for the northern peaks, while the Crawford Path heads directly north in a series of switchbacks to finally reach the windy, seemingly eternally befogged, 6,288-foot summit of Mount Washington. In fact, clouds do cover the summit 60 percent of the time and wind speeds surpass hurricane force (74 mph) about every other day. The strongest wind ever observed by man, 231 mph, was recorded here April 12, 1934. Almost nightly the temperature drops below freezing. It is possible to get snacks and hot drinks in the hut at the top. There used to be dormitory accommodations, but no longer. The only people sleeping up here are the four observers of the Mount Washington Weather Observatory, who gather data for the U.S. Weather Bureau, and four men from WMTW–TV. The weathermen live in the world's strongest building. The TV building houses transmitters for WMTW's studios in Poland Springs, Maine, as well as micro relay systems for the FBI, New Hampshire State Police, U.S. Forest Service, and Fish and Game Service and relay systems for several cable TV stations. The buildings are *out of bounds* for the throngs of tourists who come up on the railway, the Mount Washington Auto Road (toll) from Route 16, and by foot.

(By taking the Westside Trail and avoiding the summit of Mount Washington, you can save a mile and 700 feet of climbing on the hike from Lakes of the Clouds to the Madison Hut, although whichever way you choose you travel an entirely exposed route, windswept and magnificent.) From the summit of Mount Washington it is 6½ miles to the Madison Hut at 4,825 feet.

From the top I take the Gulfside Trail to the left (west), cross the tracks, then follow them a short way before heading northwest to descend through this alpine tundra on a route well marked with cairns and slashes of yellow paint, which can be followed no matter how foggy it gets. Just as the path leaves the route of the railway, the Westside Path from Lakes of the Clouds branches off to the left (south). This is the point at which one joins the Gulfside Trail when coming directly from the hut without going over the summit. A short ways farther a trail branches off to the right to go over the 5,532-

foot Mount Clay, an easy climb in good weather, with a return to the trail less than a mile away. The main trail continues down past Greenough Spring, after which it is rejoined by the Mount Clay Loop. A trail to the right soon after this junction is the Sphinx Trail, a connecting link to the Great Gulf Trail which connects with a number of trails all leading down to Route 16. Meanwhile, my trail, the Gulfside, continues on its way, crossing the grassy plateau of Monticello Lawn at 5,350 feet. (*Lawn* here means a relatively level piece of ground.) I reach the Mount Jefferson Loop (to the left— west), which goes over 5,715-foot Mount Jefferson (adding less than ½ hour to the hike, should you decide to do it), while the Gulfside climbs a little on Mount Jefferson, crosses the Six-Husbands Trail, then continues its descent past the junction where the Mount Jefferson Loop reenters it. All along the way the views are vast and powerful, but so long as I am moving most of my attention is focused down on the rough rock that requires careful stepping every mile of the route. Now the rocks descend steeply to Edmands Col (4,930 ft.) about ½ mile from the summit of Jefferson.

Trail marker on the Gulfside Trail above Edmands Col

The col divides the Connecticut and Androscoggin waters. There is a lightning-proof metal *emergency* shelter here and a bronze memorial nearby to J. Rayner Edmands, who built many of the paths in the northern peaks, including much of the Gulfside in the late nineteenth century. (The shelter is *not for camping!*) The side trails branching off the remaining 2½ miles from the col to the Madison Hut are labyrinthine. The Gulfside Trail continues its rocky way northeast, ascending from the col along a narrow ridge that separates Jefferson Ravine on the right (east) from Castle Ravine on the left, passes Adams 5, a small peak to the right, and Peabody Spring, coming in just under a mile from the hut to Thunderstorm Junction, a grassy saddle between Mounts Adams and Sam Adams, a minor summit of Mount Adams. Thunderstorm Junction is marked by the intersection of a number of trails and an enormous cairn. From here the trail descends, steeply at first, then more gently, coming to the intersection of the Air Line Trail up from Randolph. The high mountain you see northeast from here is Mount Madison. The trail continues its descent of the rocky, open slope, passes through scrub and patches of wild cranberries, and arrives at the hut.

Madison Hut to Pinkham Notch—
a little over 6 miles, about 4 hours

Leaving the hut I head east on the Osgood Trail over rock for ¼ mile, climb up a ridge a little below the summit, turn left, and arrive at the top (5,363 ft.) with its high cairn. From the summit the trail winds over the rocky, curving Osgood Ridge, marked by cairns, then descends steeply to tree line, about a mile from the summit, and continues down to about 2,500 feet and the Osgood Cut-off to the right. I follow this southwest reaching the Madison Gulf Trail in about ½ mile, cross to the southwest side of Parapet Brook, follow the ridge dividing Parapet Brook from the West Branch a short way, then turn right (southeast), come down from the ridge, cross the West Branch of the Peabody River on a bridge, continue down the steep riverbank until it levels out as the trail crosses another brook, climb easily, cross two more brooks, climb more steeply up to the next brook and up to some ledges from which I have lovely views of Mount Adams to the northwest. Going on I continue down to Lowe's Bald Spot (where a trail branches off to the left—east—to the top of this viewpoint in a few minutes) and down to the main trail to the Mount Washington Auto Road in a few minutes more. The trail comes out at the north end of a great curve in the road (marked by a 2-mile post). I cross the road, head for the south end of the curve, and pick up the Old Jackson Road which was, indeed, once a road, and follow it down a little more than 1½ miles to Pinkham Notch Camp.

(If, instead of taking the Osgood Cut-off, one were to continue straight ahead on the Osgood Trail, one would come, in about 2 miles, to Glen House. From Glen House it is possible to hike on the Aqueduct Path to 19-Mile Brook Trail directly to Carter Notch.)

Pinkham Notch Camp to Carter Notch Huts—
6¾ miles, about 6½ hours; using the
Wildcat Mountain Gondola—4½ miles,
about 3½ hours

On this route one has, amidst all the steep, rocky ascents of the White Mountains, a chance to cheat. You can take the gondola up Wildcat Mountain, cutting out 2¼ uphill miles and at least 3 hours of climbing. The gondola takes about 12½ minutes, costs $2.75 for adults, $1.50 for children under 12.

If you choose to hike, your trail—the Wildcat Ridge Trail— branches off the Lost Pond Trail, which starts across Route 16 from the parking area for Ellis Falls, not far from Pinkham Notch Camp. If you choose to travel by gondola, you must then either walk or hitch less than a mile north to the base station.

From the top of Wildcat you have a spectacular view of Mount Washington. A path from the summit terminal leads to the observation tower from which you have a view to the east as well as all that

Carter Notch Hut

to the west. From the tower the trail continues on to Summit D. (There are a series of cols and summits, some lettered, some not, on this route, so that even with the gondola ride you have a nice day's worth of ups and downs.) At Summit D the path descends into Wildcat Col, climbs out of it, over another, slightly higher col, then climbs the long ridge to Peak C, then another col, another rise, a climb up through woods to Summit B, and then, about 2½ miles from the top station of the gondola, the trail comes to the main summit at 4,397 feet, the highest point on this many-peaked mountain. Shortly beyond this the trail descends very steeply for almost a mile, down through woods over huge boulders, coming to the junction of 19-Mile Brook Trail. Turning right (south) at the junction, the trail soon comes to the two lovely lakes of Carter Notch and the small, charming old stone hut (3,400 feet). Built in 1914, the hut is used as the dining room and crew quarters, while two separate bunkhouses built in the 1960s house guests behind the hut.

The weather has been clear, perfect, and now, late in the day, is turning cold. Along the way the green mountainsides were dotted with trees of brilliant red, like flames leaping up; perfect, individual, contained flames. I hate to think of this trip ending.

Carter Notch Huts to Glen House—
3½ miles, about 1¾ hours

I leave early in the morning for the short walk out on the 19-Mile Brook Trail past the lakes and the junction of the Wildcat Ridge Trail to the left and on down the wide, comfortable path through woods, crossing a stream after about 1½ miles and continuing on through woods to cross another brook, soon after which the Carter Dome Trail to Zeta Pass on the Carter-Moriah Trail branches off to the right (east). The 19-Mile Brook Trail continues straight ahead, the brook itself a marvel of rushing water a little below the trail on the left. About 2½ miles after leaving the hut I arrive at the junction of the Aqueduct Path, which leads in less than a mile to Glen House on the left. The turn-off is easy to miss, but is just below a dam, 0.6 mile after the Carter Dome Trail junction. It crosses the brook below the dam, turns left, and continues level to the aqueduct which it follows, descending ¼ mile as it approaches Glen House. If you miss the trail, the 19-Mile Brook Trail is prettier anyway. It continues along the brook a little more than a mile before coming to Route 16, about a mile north of Glen House and less than 2½ miles north of Pinkham Notch.

∧∧∧

Hiking in the White Mountains is for experienced hikers eager for the challenge of a steep, rocky, difficult world where the distances are long and the weather can be abominable. In August 1976, for instance, I hiked in a blizzard from Mizpah Springs Hut to Lakes of the Clouds. Winds of more than 60 miles an hour drove tiny ice crystals into my eyes, the only part of me I couldn't cover up, and the wind itself sometimes knocked me off balance. But I did have winter gear with me and I found the storm exhilarating. Nevertheless, only one other party was equipped to make that hike that day—all the others turned back. At Lakes the water pipes froze and parts of the radio antenna were broken off by the heavy ice, falling, crashing onto the roof. The following morning, brilliantly clear, 26°F with a wind-chill factor of −7°, the entire world shimmered under a coating of ice. As I mentioned earlier, these are the most difficult of any of the hikes in this book, except for the steep snow in Colorado and the Tetons. But there are 1,126.1 miles of trails in White Mountain National Forest (including those in Maine). Some of them are easier than those between the huts, and as noted in the beginning of this chapter, so are some trails *to* the huts from places other than other huts. For example, from the trailhead on the road it is an easy hike along the 19-Mile Brook Trail to Carter Notch Hut, or, via the trail from Lafayette Place, it is equally easy to Lonesome Lake Hut. This hut was left out of my route, but it is also maintained by the AMC. Even Madison Hut can be reached by the easy and pro-tected Valley Way (steep only at its end) from the Appalachia parking area on Route 2 between Lowe's Store and Randolph.

All of the trails, easy or challenging, offer a glimpse into a unique, rough, and extraordinary world. I think it would be nice to hike every mile of them.

PART THREE

ECOLOGICAL EPILOGUE

*"A splendid place for people,
but only for a few at a time"* *

Time exists wherever the world is in balance. Where the land still has a past that has continued over eons to this day, it has a future. Where we have tampered with it, destroying the ecological balance of it, it has no history. It has only this moment to which we have brought it. To protect Time, we preserve wilderness.

The fact that the feet, tents, fires, and waste of backpackers are more than the land can endure may seem preposterous in the light of the numbers of avalanches, landslides, earthquakes, glaciers, volcanos, forest fires, floods, winds, and various weathers to which it has already been subjected. But each person's feet and habits, as one set in a series of thousands, unnaturally and vitally alter the surface of each small piece of this fragile earth and, therefore, the ecological balance, the history, of that place.

It was the middle of the nineteenth century when it first occured to us that preservation was a necessity. In this last half of the twentieth, our desperation and the ever-widening extent of our awareness have produced highly organized preservationist groups.

* John Mitchell in *Losing Ground,* Sierra Club Books, San Francisco, 1975.

239

And some results. Nearly a century's work culminated in the passing of the Wilderness Act of 1964, a real recognition of wilderness by our government that extended beyond the establishment of National Parks to form the National Wilderness Preservation System. It included 9.1 million acres of National Forest land, 0.4 percent of America.

But the act also ordered studies of all tracts of roadless, contiguous land of at least 5,000 acres to see if they should be included in the system. And it provided us with a technical definition of wilderness: ". . . federal land retaining its primeval character and influence, without permanent improvements or human habitation . . ."

Three agencies administer wilderness: The Forest Service of the U.S. Department of Agriculture, and the National Park Service and the Fish and Wildlife Service, both under the aegis of the U.S. Department of the Interior.

While the order to study all lands of at least 5,000 acres did not preclude studying smaller tracts of land, it did make it possible legally to ignore smaller, equally wild land. From the beginning of its wilderness management, only the Fish and Wildlife Service, which currently administers thirty-six wilderness areas consisting of 575,620 acres, included small areas in its many tiny, roadless islands. But the Forest Service has recently formed three wilderness areas under 5,000 acres. They are all in the East, where large tracts of undisturbed land are rarer than in the West. Bristol Cliffs' 3,775 acres are part of Green Mountain National Forest in Vermont; Gee Creek's 2,570 acres belong to Tennessee's Cherokee National Forest; and the 3,600 acres of Ellicott Rock sit at the common junction of North Carolina, South Carolina, and Georgia.

The bulk of our wilderness—87 areas comprising 11,981,424 acres—lies within the 154 National Forests (which include mountains as well as trees) managed by the U.S. Forest Service.

More wilderness is coming. Pending before Congress are 20 proposals involving 3.8 million acres of Forest Service land; 41 proposals involving 14.8 million acres of National Park land; and 49 proposals involving 7.5 million acres of Fish and Wildlife Service land. Within specific parks, the National Park Service has lumped together, under one name, some noncontiguous wilderness areas under 5,000 acres.

Two hundred sixty other areas, about 12 million acres, are still being studied to determine which of them should be proposed for wilderness classification.

Once the 110 proposals now pending are incorporated into the Wilderness Preservation System, 26.1 million acres will be added to the 12,757,989 acres of our current 127 wilderness areas. How much of America, which not awfully long ago was 100 percent wild, does it come to? About 1.6 percent.

Technical wilderness is not the only place where land is preserved. A preservationist philosophy is basically at work in the country's thirty-seven National Parks, even though they contain, at this moment before the pending proposals have been approved, only four wilderness areas comprising 200,945 acres. While everything in National Parks—land, water, vegetation, animals—is protected, it is nevertheless a protected environment that does not meet all the criteria of the Wilderness Act, which prohibits roads, hotels, stores, resorts, summer homes, camps, hunting and fishing lodges, motor boats, airplane landings, and commercial lumbering. (The Wilderness Act does allow hunting, fishing, and mineral exploration and mining, although hunting is prohibited in National Parks.)

The National Park System (which includes recreational and historical areas as well as strictly natural areas) consists of 30 million acres, or about 0.1 percent of the country. A proposed 32 million acres of land in Alaska, to be turned over to the National Park Service, would double that percentage.

Botswana has allocated 13.6 percent of its land for National Parks. President Mobutu of Zaire has announced a plan to expand Zaire's National Parks to cover 12 to 15 percent of the country. But then, that's another world.

A LITTLE SOLITUDE, MAYBE

The well-paved roads of National Parks bring in millions of tourists annually. Thousands leave their cars to head for the well-marked trails of the backcountry. (Backcountry can be defined as undeveloped land, technical wilderness or not, at least ½ mile from roads open to the public for use by wheeled vehicles.) Backpackers stream into wilderness areas of National Forests as well. Still, large areas of the backcountry are not yet overused. In some National Forests, where hiking trails are not so well marked and maintained as in National Parks, it is possible to hike for days and see hardly a soul.

There are even National Parks where, for all the cars, backpackers on the trails are sparse. In Yellowstone and Glacier National Parks many hikers are simply afraid of the grizzlies. (It is not irrational to be afraid of a grizzly.) But whoever hikes there has magnificent backcountry largely to himself, not to mention the possibility of *seeing* one of these threatened beasts.

Conversely, National Forests are not always free of crowds. Some, like White River National Forest near Aspen, or the White Mountain National Forest in New Hampshire, are every bit as overused as most National Parks.

EXPERIMENTS

In overused areas, in order to keep large portions of park or forest from being destroyed, there has been in recent years a trend toward consolidating camping in specific backcountry sites. This has produced trampled, littered suburbs of tents and lines of campers in front of the outhouse. When I asked a ranger in Olympic National Park if I *must* camp at a campsite she said, sadly, "No . . . if you don't mind trampling grass that hasn't already been trampled."

But so much damage has been done to some of these sites that they have been closed to camping to allow them to regenerate, a process the Park Service estimates takes two seasons. While currently less than 1 percent of the total number of campsites are closed, that low figure is due both to more restrictive measures for the users of the backcountry and to the use of other approaches that try to spread campers out a bit, specifically to keep all the trampling from happening in one place—regardless of the sad-eyed lady of Olympic.

Grand Teton National Park, as I mentioned earlier, often uses camping zones rather than specific sites and puts a tight limit on the number of campers allowed in each zone. For the camper this can necessitate making reservations months in advance. The Tetons are not alone in virtually requiring reservations for anyone with a specific route in mind. In almost every popular area, reservations for campsites or shelter space are the only insurance that you will be able to make the hike you want.

Shenandoah National Park is currently experimenting with dispersing campers away from *any* specific sites or zones. Campers are no longer even allowed to camp at shelters which are now kept locked, although they are opened by rangers in case of extremely bad weather. It is illegal to camp within view of a shelter or of other campers. This seems more in the spirit of the outdoors than the crowded campsites, but Shenandoah is a fairly small park—96 miles long and only 13–16 miles wide. It is easily reached for overnight trips by even the most inexperienced campers from the Blue Ridge Parkway which bisects it. With a rather large number of hikers, this system may ultimately bog down when campers in every ideal spot are careless with waste and garbage over a period of time.

TWO MEANS TOWARD AN END

The efforts of the Park Service, concerned with keeping the backcountry from being overcrowded, are not subtle. The camper bears his share of maintaining the quality of the wilderness experience by letting go a part of it in order to stick to a specific schedule and route. When he fills out his backcountry permit he trades his regular city or town schedule for a new one—one that just happens to take place in the wilds.

The philosophy of the Forest Service, on the other hand, is that the wilderness experience should not be *visibly* subject to control. Then it runs the gamut of systems—from requiring no permit at all to requiring a permit just to enter for a day hike. Where there is a need to regulate numbers in a wilderness area, the Forest Service prefers to do it subtly if it can, by regulating the numbers of people who enter a wilderness area (possibly at one trailhead but not at another), then allowing them to experience a backcountry free of restrictions other than those of camping a certain number of feet from a stream or trail.

Either way, it is no longer possible for people to experience the wilderness as they would have a hundred years ago. But the restrictions, blatant or subtle, will at least allow wilderness to exist a hundred years from now.

A THIRD MEANS

One effective way of taking pressure off the land is through hut systems. Such systems are proven protectors of the environment in the fragile landscape of the high Alps. The ugliness of the tent suburbs would be dispelled by huts. If all sleeping, eating, and waste were concentrated in one spot, the landscape would be free of all traces of campsites—fireplaces, charred earth, half-burned cans, forgotten garbage, flattened grass. A simple structure, a hut stands as the single interruption on a landscape that remains pristine. And huts, built of natural materials, are certainly far less an interruption of the landscape than myriad multicolored, rip-stop-nylon tents.

There are two standard arguments against huts. They are usually delivered vociferously. One is that huts will lure even more people into the backcountry. In the huts that already exist—those in the White Mountains, the tent-hotels in Yosemite, and the occasional others elsewhere—one meets many older, experienced hikers, knowledgeable and responsible about the outdoors, who prefer not to carry 40-pound packs on their backs. These people are noticeably missing at campsites filled with the young and strong. But huts (both here and in the Alps) are often located at the end of difficult and challenging trails, hardly the terrain to attract the feared hordes of novice hikers.

And even if new hikers *are* attracted to the backcountry, they only add to the number of potential voices there are to raise in the salvation of the acres and acres of unprotected backcountry that still exist.

The second argument is that *any* structure is inconsistent with wilderness. Are densely populated campsites consistent? In fact, any permanent structure *is* inconsistent with the *definition of wilderness* in the Wilderness Act. But huts need not be built in wilderness areas. They can do just as much, or more, toward protecting the environment if they are built throughout the remaining backcountry.

So, for that matter, can shelters. The shelters in most parks and forests are old, dating back to the 1920s and 1930s. A large number of them were built by the Civilian Conservation Corps— that is, they were products of the depression. Today many of them are in something of a depression themselves, attacked by time and vandals. The tendency of the National Parks is to remove them. The logic behind that is that when the shelters were built, tents weighed 20 pounds. Now that tents weigh 6 pounds, shelters are unnecessary, although the Park Service says it would not hesitate to recommend shelters, even in wilderness areas, if shelters are desirable. (Since shelters do not have foundations, the Park Service does not think of them as permanent structures.) They believe shelters are desirable only under certain circumstances—in Alaska, for instance, where one encounters incredible weather and many bears.

The real reason for removing the shelters is that although permits are issued in accordance with shelter capacity, there are still great numbers of people *without* permits camping in the shelter areas. The Park Service believes that removing the shelters will relieve the burden on the shelter sites. But how? Taking a shelter away doesn't seem to me to provide a guard against illegal camping.

A better plan might be to follow the example of the Appalachian Mountain Club and the U.S. Forest Service in the White Mountain National Forest. Together they have taken energetic action to clean up shelter sites that had become virtual slums, repairing and rebuilding shelters and toilets, erecting tent platforms, and, in some cases, charging small fees and assigning resident caretakers.

Their concept is diversity. Everything should exist—undesignated campsites where the individual camper leaves no trace of ever having been there; campsite facilities with shelters, tent platforms, toilets, fire grates, resident caretakers; and huts. The presence of a caretaker is a gentle, powerful enforcer—a superb guard against illegal camping as well as a source of information. In areas other than the White Mountains, couldn't such programs be carried out with local hiking clubs working with specific parks or forests?

In the European countries, huts are maintained by their respective alpine clubs, but open to all hikers, without reservations. Sleeping is cheap and what you eat, and therefore how much you spend, is your own choice. You are also free to bring your own food. The huts must meet certain government standards in both the quality and the price of the services offered, so there is no possibility of them becoming high-altitude McDonald's. There is not much incentive for the kind of profit-oriented concessioners to whom we willingly submit.

Does the Music Corporation of America really belong in a National Park? In 1973 MCA paid $7.2 million to add the Yosemite Park and Curry Company to its list of more than sixty subsidiaries. So it is MCA that currently maintains the High Sierra Camps as well as hotels in the valley. In other parks TWA, General Foods, and AMFAC play similar roles. So long as big corporations are involved, the simplicity, philosophy, and cost of huts—or any lodging or services—is questionable. The government standards in Europe ensure that the huts retain a simple mountain atmosphere. Big business certainly doesn't.

There has been talk of moving *all* concessions outside park boundaries. That was, in fact, one of the recommendations made by the same Symposium on National Parks for the Future mentioned in Part One. It would be an effective way of drawing into the parks only those people who were actually interested in the parks for their natural qualities. Mountain huts, maintained by the hiking and conservation clubs working with the Park and Forest Services, run on a nonprofit basis, and accessible only by foot or by horse, could replace the current concession-run lodging along with overused backcountry campsites.

Huts do not require the building of roads. Food and supplies can be brought up on the backs of men, as in the AMC huts in the White Mountains, or by horse or mule, as in Yosemite. The helicopters that are used to airlift out the portable containers from campsite outhouses could airlift *in* necessary building materials. In many cases ranger cabins could form the core at least if not the whole, of a hut.

At the trailhead of a path up to a hut in Austria I found a pile of bricks and a sign asking each hiker who passed to carry one or two up so the hut could build additional sleeping space. Slow—but in the Alps there is time.

PART FOUR

APPENDIXES

Appendix A   Books

Sierra Club Totebooks for the states mentioned:

Climber's Guide to Yosemite Valley, Steve Roper. ($7.15)

Hikers' Guide to the Smokies, Dick Murlless and Constance Stallings. Maps. ($7.95)

Hiking the Bigfoot Country: The Wildlands of Northern California and Southern Oregon, John Hart. Maps. ($7.95)

Hiking the Teton Backcountry, Paul Lawrence. Maps. ($4.95)

Hiking the Yellowstone Backcountry, Orville Bach. Maps. ($4.95)

Mountaineers Guide to the High Sierra, edited by Hervey Voge and Andrew J. Smatko. ($7.95)

Reading the Rocks: A Layman's Guide to the Geologic Secrets of Canyons, Mesas and Buttes of the American Southwest, David A. Rahm. Photos and diagrams. ($7.95)

Starr's Guide to the John Muir Trail and the High Sierra Region, Walter A. Starr, Jr. Map and mileage chart. ($3.95)

251

Totebooks helpful in any region:

The Best about Backpacking, edited by Denise Van Lear. ($6.95)

Cooking for Camp and Trail, Hasse Bunnelle with Shirley Sarvis. ($3.95)

Fieldbook of Nature Photography, edited by Patricia Maye. ($6.95)

Food for Knapsackers, Hasse Bunnelle. ($3.95)

Books particularly helpful to the novice backpacker:

Backpacking, R. C. Rethmel. Burgess Publishing Co., 7108 Ohms Lane, Minneapolis, Minnesota 55435 ($4.50 paperback)

Backpacking Equipment: A Consumer's Guide, William Kemsley, Jr., and the editors of *Backpacker* magazine. Macmillan Publishing Co., New York. ($4.95 paperback)

Backpacking: One Step at a Time, Harvey Manning. Vintage Books, New York. ($2.95 paperback)

The New Complete Walker, Colin Fletcher. Alfred A. Knopf, New York. ($10.00 hardcover)

Pleasure Packing: How to Backpack in Comfort, Robert Wood. Condor Books, 1736 Stockton Street, San Francisco, California 94133. ($3.95 paperback)

An assortment of other books and publications:

Two concerns with a large mail-order business have highly informative catalogs that you might also find helpful. Eastern Mountain Sports (EMS), 1041 Commonwealth Avenue, Boston, Massachusetts 02215, will send you their catalog for $1.00 or free with an order. Recreational Equipment, Inc. (REI), 1525 11th Avenue, Seattle, Washington 98122, is a co-op that you may join for $2.00 plus a yearly purchase of at least $5.00. Dividends are based on the amount of your purchases. It is not necessary to be a co-op member, however, to buy from them.

Camping (in National Forests), pamphlet PA–502, Superintendent of Documents, U.S. Government Printing Office, Washington, D.C. 20402. (25¢)

Camping in the National Park System, pamphlet S/N 2405–0205, Superintendent of Documents, U.S. Government Printing Office, Washington, D.C. 20402 (25¢)

A Guide to the National Parks, Their Landscape and Geology, William H. Matthews III, Doubleday/Natural History Press, New York. ($5.95 paperback)

The Handbook of Wilderness Travel, George S. Wells. Colorado Outdoor Sports Corp., 5450 North Valley Highway, Denver, Colorado 80216. ($3.75 paperback)

The Hiker's Bible, Robert Elman. Doubleday & Co., New York. ($2.50 paperback)

Introduction to Foot Trails in America, Robert Colwell. Stackpole Books, Cameron and Kelker Streets, Harrisburg, Pennsylvania 17105. ($3.95 paperback)

Lightweight Equipment for Hiking, Camping and Mountaineering, Potomac Appalachian Trail Club, 1718 N Street, N.W., Washington, D.C. 20036. ($1.00 paperback) This is a frequently updated listing of equipment with descriptions, prices, and sources and is most useful to backpackers without easy access to a well-stocked mountaineering shop.

Mountaineering Medicine, Fred T. Darvill, Jr., M.D. Skagit Mountain Rescue Unit, P.O. Box 2, Mt. Vernon, Washington 98273. ($1.00 paperback)

Open Lands Project Listing of Trails Pamphlets, Open Lands Project, 53 W. Jackson Boulevard, Chicago, Illinois 60604. ($1.00) This is an informally organized listing of groups to write to for information on hiking (and bicycle, canoe, ski, motorcycle) trails, as well as a listing of guide books and their prices for the same activities.

Outdoor Living: Problems, Solutions, Guidelines, edited by Eugene H. Fear. Tacoma Unit, Mountain Rescue Council, c/o Everett Lasher, P.O. Box 696, Tacoma, Washington 98401. ($2.50 paperback)

Rand McNally National Forest Guide, Len Hilts. ($4.95 paperback) Not primarily for hikers, but useful for general tourist information, including recreation possibilities and historical information.

Rand McNally Natonal Park Guide, Michael Frome. ($4.95 paperback) Not aimed at hikers, but provides practical information about access, lodging, special programs, etc.

Wilderness Areas of North America, Ann and Myron Sutton. Funk & Wagnalls, New York. ($4.95 paperback)

The Wilderness Route Finder, Calvin Rutstrum. Macmillan Publishing Co., New York. ($1.50 paperback)

Wilderness Survival, Berndt Berglund. Charles Scribner's Sons, New York. ($2.95 paperback) This includes information on first aid, shelters, cooking, edible plants, hunting and fishing, use of map and compass, fire building, etc.

Guides to campgrounds:

Camper's Favorite Campgrounds: The East Coast from Maine to Florida, Joseph Steinberg. Dial Press, New York. ($7.95 paperback) It covers only selected campgrounds, but serves as an informative, pleasant travel guide for the areas around them.

Rand McNally Campground and Trailer Park Guide. ($6.95 paperback) Published annually, it covers the U.S., Canada, and Mexico.

Woodall's Trailering Parks and Campgrounds, distributed by Simon & Schuster, New York. Two volumes are published: East ($4.95 paperback) and West ($2.95 paperback).

Appendix B   National Forests and Parks of the states in this book

Following are lists of the National Forests and the National Parks. For information about specific National Forests and the wilderness areas within them, write to the regional headquarters. For information about the specific National Parks, write to the addresses listed below. Listings are in the order of the tours described in the book.

WASHINGTON

Forest Service Regional Headquarters
Pacific Northwest Region
P.O. Box 3623
319 S.W. Pine Street
Portland, Oregon 97208

 Colville National Forest, Colville
 Gifford Pinchot National Forest, Vancouver
 Mount Baker National Forest, Bellingham
 Okanogan National Forest, Okanogan
 Olympic National Forest, Olympia

Snoqualmie National Forest, Seattle
Wenatchee National Forest, Wenatchee

Mount Rainier National Park, Longmire 98397
North Cascades National Park, Sedro Woolley 98284
Olympic National Park, 600 East Park Avenue, Port Angeles 98362

CALIFORNIA

Forest Service Regional Headquarters
California Region
630 Sansome Street
San Francisco, California 94111

Angeles National Forest, Pasadena
Calveras Bigtree National Forest, Sonora
Cleveland National Forest, San Diego
Eldorado National Forest, Placerville
Inyo National Forest, Bishop
Klamath National Forest, Yreka
Lassen National Forest, Susanville
Los Padres National Forest, Santa Barbara
Mendocino National Forest, Willows
Modoc National Forest, Alturas
Plumas National Forest, Quincy
San Bernardino National Forest, San Bernardino
Sequoia National Forest, Porterville
Shasta-Trinity National Forests (two separate forests under one
supervisor), Redding
Sierra National Forest, Fresno
Six Rivers National Forest, Eureka
Stanislaus National Forest, Sonora
Tahoe National Forest, Nevada City

Kings Canyon National Park, Three Rivers 93271
Lassen Volcanic National Park, Mineral 96063
Redwood National Park, Drawer N, Crescent City 95531
Sequoia National Park, Three Rivers 93271
Yosemite National Park, P.O. Box 577, Yosemite National Park
95389

COLORADO

Forest Service Regional Headquarters
Rocky Mountain Region
Federal Center, Building 85
Denver, Colorado 80225

>Arapaho National Forest, Golden
>Grand Mesa–Uncompahgre National Forests (two separate forests under one supervisor), Delta
>Gunnison National Forest, Gunnison
>Pike National Forest, Colorado Springs
>Rio Grande National Forest, Monte Vista
>Roosevelt National Forest, Fort Collins
>Routt National Forest, Steamboat Springs
>San Isabel National Forest, Pueblo
>San Juan National Forest, Durango
>White River National Forest, Glenwood Springs

Mesa Verde National Park, Mesa Verde National Park 81330 (no backpacking—hiking only with a uniformed National Park Service guide)
Rocky Mountain National Park, Estes Park 80517

WYOMING

Wyoming is administered by two regional offices:
Forest Service Regional Headquarters
Rocky Mountain Region
Federal Center, Building 85
Denver, Colorado 80225

>Bighorn National Forest, Sheridan
>Medicine Bow National Forest, Laramie
>Shoshone National Forest, Cody

Forest Service Regional Headquarters
Intermountain Region
324 25th Street
Ogden, Utah 84401

Bridger National Forest, Kemmerer
Teton National Forest, Jackson

Grand Teton National Park, P.O. Box 67, Moose 83012
Yellowstone National Park, Yellowstone National Park 82190

MINNESOTA, MICHIGAN, AND NEW HAMPSHIRE

Minnesota, Michigan, and New Hampshire are all administered by:
Forest Service Regional Headquarters
Eastern Region
633 West Wisconsin Avenue
Milwaukee, Wisconsin 53203

Michigan:
Hiawatha National Forest, Escanaba
Huron National Forest, Cadillac
Manistee National Forest, Cadillac
Ottawa National Forest, Ironwood

Isle Royale National Park, 87 North Ripley Street, Houghton 49931

Minnesota:
Chippewa National Forest, Cass Lake
Superior National Forest, Duluth

New Hampshire:
White Mountain National Forest, Laconia

NORTH CAROLINA AND TENNESSEE

North Carolina and Tennessee are both administered by:
Forest Service Regional Headquarters
Southern Region
1720 Peachtree Road, N.W.
Atlanta, Georgia 30309

For information about the following North Carolina forests, write to:
National Forests in North Carolina
P.O. Box 731
Asheville 28802

Croatan National Forest
Nantahala National Forest
Pisgah National Forest
Uwharrie National Forest

Tennessee:
Cherokee National Forest, Cleveland
Great Smoky Mountains National Park, Gatlinburg 37738

Two other National Parks mentioned in this book:

Glacier National Park, West Glacier, Montana 59936
Shenandoah National Park, Luray, Virginia 22835

NATIONAL HEADQUARTERS

U.S. Forest Service
Department of Agriculture
14th Street and Independence Avenue, S.W.
Washington, D.C. 20250

National Park Service
Department of the Interior
C Street between 18th and 19th Streets, N.W.
Washington, D.C. 20240

Appendix C Lodging within the National Parks of the tours

OLYMPIC NATIONAL PARK, WASHINGTON

Kalaloch Beach Ocean Village (lodge rooms, motel, housekeeping cabins, dining room, bar, grocery). Open all year.
Write: Manager, Route 1, Clearwater, Washington 98399. *Phone:* (206) 962-2271.

Lake Crescent Lodge (lodge rooms and cottages, dining room, bar). Memorial Day through Labor Day. Accessible by bus from Port Angeles.
Write: National Park Concessions, Inc., Star Route 1, Port Angeles, Washington 98362. *Phone:* (206) 928-3211.

Lake Crescent Log Cabin Resort (housekeeping cabins, lunch counter, groceries, trailer parking). April to October.
Write: Manager, Route 1, Box 416, Port Angeles, Washington 98362. *Phone:* (206) 928-3245.

La Push Ocean Park (housekeeping cabins). Open all year.
Write: Manager, La Push, Washington 98350. *Phone:* (206) 374-5267.

Sol Duc Hot Springs (cabins, motel units, lodge rooms, swimming pool, dining room, bar, grocery). May through September.
Write: National Park Concessions, Inc., Star Route 1, Port Angeles, Washington 98362. *Phone:* (206) 928-3211.

YOSEMITE NATIONAL PARK, CALIFORNIA

In the high country, besides Tuolumne Meadows Lodge and the High Sierra Camps, there is White Wolf Lodge, midway between the Valley and Tuolumne Meadows and accessible by road. Other lodging and restaurants exist in the Valley, at Wawona and El Portal. For information about all of it, write: Yosemite Park and Curry Co., Yosemite National Park, California 95389.

GRAND TETON NATIONAL PARK, WYOMING

Colter Bay Village, Jackson Lake Lodge, and Jenny Lake Lodge are all operated by:
The Grand Teton Lodge Co., P.O. Box 240, Moran, Wyoming 83013. *Phone:* (307) 733-2811.
or telephone directly: Colter Bay Village and Jackson Lake Lodge— (307) 543-2855, Jenny Lake Lodge—(307) 733-4647.

Colter Bay Cabins, Tent Village, Trailer Park (cafeteria and grill, bar, shops, horses). Rates (double occupancy): in cabins, $12.00– $33.00 per day, end of May to October; in canvas and log tents with woodburning stove and double bunks, $8.00 per day, end of June to Labor Day; in trailer park, $5.00 per day.

Jackson Lake Lodge (lodge rooms, motel units, dining room, shops, swimming pool, horses). Rates (double occupancy): $26.00–$42.00 per day, European plan. Mid-June to Labor Day.

Jenny Lake Lodge (one- and two-room cabins, dining room, horses). Rates (double occupancy): $75.00–$125.00 per day, modified American plan. June to mid-September.

Grand Teton Climbers Ranch (bunk space, cooking shelter, and showers for registered climbers). June through September.

Write: P.O. Box 157, Moose, Wyoming 83012. *Phone:* (307) 733-4496.
or: American Alpine Club, 113 East 90th Street, New York, New York 10028.

Leek's Lodge (cabins). May through September. Moran, Wyoming 83013. *Phone:* (307) 543-2494.

Signal Mountain Lodge (lodge, cabins, housekeeping apartments, dining room, grocery). Open all year. Moran, Wyoming 83013. *Phone:* (307) 543-2831.

Triangle X Ranch (cabins, dining room, horses). American plan. Open all year. Moose, Wyoming 83012. *Phone:* (307) 733-2183.

The preceding are all park concessioners. There are other accommodations, including a number of dude ranches, on private property within the park boundaries but not subject to the regulations of the National Park Service. For a list of these places, write Park Headquarters.

ISLE ROYALE NATIONAL PARK, MICHIGAN

Rock Harbor Lodge (lodge rooms—American plan—and housekeeping units). Third Saturday in June through Labor Day. *Write:* P.O. Box 405, Houghton, Michigan 49931. *Phone:* (906) 482-2890.
or, for information out of season, *write:* National Park Concessions, Inc., Mammoth Cave, Kentucky 42259. *Phone:* (502) 758-2217.

GREAT SMOKY MOUNTAINS NATIONAL PARK, TENNESSEE—NORTH CAROLINA

Le Conte Lodge (cabins, dining room). Mid-April to late October. Accessible only by foot or by horse, although there are no accommodations for horses, which must be taken back down to their stables by a guide. Horses are available from McCarter's or Smokey Mountain Riding Stables (see pp. 265–66).
Write: Le Conte Lodge, Inc., P.O. Box 350, Gatlinburg, Tennessee

37738. *Phone:* (615) 436-4473, 9:00 A.M. to 4:00 P.M., Monday through Friday.

GLACIER NATIONAL PARK, MONTANA

Sperry Chalet and *Granite Park Chalet,* both accessible by foot or horseback.
Write: Belton Chalets, Inc., Box 188, West Glacier, Montana 59936.
Phone: (406) 888-5511.
For other accommodations in the park, *write:* Glacier Park, Inc., East Glacier Park, Montana 59434.
or, out of season (mid-September to mid-May), *write:* Glacier Park, Inc., P.O. Box 4340, Tucson, Arizona 85717.

Appendix D Pack stock

There are a number of conservation organizations that sponsor guided pack trips and walking trips with pack stock. Some of these may coincide with areas in this book. For further information, write:

National Wildlife Federation
1412 16th Street N.W.
Washington, D.C. 20036

The American Forestry Association
1319 18th Street N.W.
Washington, D.C. 20036

The Wilderness Society
729 15th Street N.W.
Washington, D.C. 20005

All three organizations will send you a brochure about their trips. The Sierra Club, 530 Bush Street, San Francisco, California 94108, also organizes a few guided pack trips.

As for the areas in the book:
Olympic National Park: A list of packers and regulations for travel with stock is available from the park superintendent. There are no stables in the park.

Yosemite National Park: Saddle and pack animals are available at stables in Yosemite Valley, White Wolf, Tuolumne Meadows, Wawona, and Mather. Guided half-day and full-day trips as well as tours of several days are possible. The entire High Sierra Circuit can be done as a guided trip by horse or mule. Contact Yosemite Park and Curry Co., Yosemite National Park, California 95389.

Uncompahgre National Forest: For a list of packers in the San Juan–Uncompahgre region, contact the Forest Supervisor, 11th and Main Street, Delta, Colorado 81416, or try outfitter Emmet C. Koppenhafer, 320 South Market, Cortez, Colorado 81321.

Grand Teton National Park: There are stables at Colter Bay Village, Jackson Lake Lodge, Jenny Lake Lodge, and Teton Village with guided trips of an hour to several days. Contact park headquarters, or for information in winter, call: (208) 624-7956 (St. Anthony, Idaho). The Wyoming Outfitters Association, Box A1, Jackson, Wyoming 83001, can provide you with a list of other outfitters in the area.

Isle Royale National Park: The only hooved animals in the park are moose, which cannot be hired. Alternate transportation to foot here means boats: either canoes, which cannot be rented on the island but can be brought over on the boat, or motor boats. Rentals, tours, and charters are available at Rock Harbor Lodge.

Great Smoky Mountains National Park:
McCarter's Riding Stables
Twomile Branch
Gatlinburg, Tennessee 37738 (near park headquarters)

Smoky Mountains Riding Stables
Box 445
Gatlinburg, Tennessee 37738 (about 2 miles east of town)

Cades Cove Riding Stables
Cades Cove
Star Route
Townsend, Tennessee 37882

Smokemont Riding Stables
Cherokee, North Carolina 28719 (near Smokemont Campground)

Cosby Stables
E. G. Bryant
Route 2
Newport, Tennessee 37821 (operated out of Cosby Campground)

You can make a tour of any number of days by horse. Almost every campsite has a hitching rack.

White Mountain National Forest: Not exactly horse country. The best alternative to walking here is in winter when you can ski cross-country. The town of Jackson, just down Route 16 from Pinkham Notch, has one of the most extensive systems of ski touring trails in the country, to which the Wildcat Ridge Trail connects. For more information, write: Jackson Ski Touring Center, Jackson, New Hampshire 03846.

Appendix E   Entrance fees

Some National Parks (and National Monuments, Recreation Areas, Seashores, Historic and Memorial Parks administered by the National Park Service) charge entrance fees. As of this writing, only two tours in this book are in such areas; those in Yosemite and the Tetons, and if you start your hike via the tram to Rendezvous Mountain in the Tetons, you do not pay a fee. (The fee would be less than the tram ticket, however.) Where fees are charged they are usually somewhere between $2.00 and $3.00 per car.

An annual permit, the Golden Eagle Passport, is available for $10.00. It covers entrance fees for the permittee and anyone accompanying him or her for one calendar year. It is not a bargain unless you plan numerous trips into areas charging entrance fees. For U.S. citizens or residents 62 or older, a lifetime Golden Age Passport is available without charge. It admits the permittee and any people accompanying him. It also provides a 50 percent discount on camping or other fees for designated recreational facilities and services (but not on charges made by private concessioners or contractors operating within federal areas). It must be applied for in person with proof of age and can be obtained at National Park Headquarters in Washington, regional offices, and areas of the National Park System where entrance fees are charged; and at Forest Service Headquarters in Washington, regional offices, Forest Supervisors' offices, and ranger stations of the Forest Service (although there are no fees as of this writing to enter any Forest Service lands). The Golden Eagle Passport can be obtained at the same places or by mail. It does not provide any discounts.

Appendix F Addresses of freeze-dried food distributors

Camplite, 40 East 2430 South, Salt Lake City, Utah 84115

Chuck Wagon Foods, Box 226, Woburn, Massachusetts 01801

Dri-Lite Foods, 11333 South Atlantic, Lynwood, California 90264

Freeze-Dry Foods Ltd., 201 Savings Bank Building, Ithaca, N.Y. 14850 or 579 Speers Road, Oarville, Ontario, Canada

National Package Foods (Seidel Trail Packets), 632 East 185th Street, Cleveland, Ohio 44119

Oregon Freeze-Dry Foods, Inc., P.O. Box 666, Albany, Oregon 97321 *

* Oregon Freeze-Dry Foods produces both Mountain House and Tea Kettle. It is the only company in this list that will not sell to you directly, but it will provide you with a list of retailers in your area. All of these companies will send you a list of their products, some faster than others. In ordering food from any of them, allow plenty of time for delivery, which can sometimes take up to a month. In some cases you get a discount on large orders. Unopened, freeze-dried foods keep for years, so order extra if you backpack often. But don't order large amounts of anything you haven't tasted.

Rich-Moor Lite Weight Camp Food, P.O. Box 2728, Van Nuys, California 98122

Stow-Lite, 166 Cushing Highway, Cohasset, Massachusetts 02025

Trail Chef, 2140 51st Street, Los Angeles, California 90015

Wilsons & Co., 4545 North Lincoln Boulevard, Oklahoma City, Oklahoma 73105

ABOUT THE AUTHOR

Ruth Rudner is an experienced backpacker who loves to wander and explore the wild country of Europe and America. She lived in Austria where she worked in 1964 as a contributing editor for *Ski* magazine. Since moving to the United States, she has continued yearly trips to Europe, usually spending several months in the Alps. She has bicycled from Austria to Yugoslavia, and in Germany's Black Forest from Freiburg to Baden-Baden. In addition to hiking, climbing, skiing, and bicycling, Miss Rudner has raced cars on an ice track above the Arctic Circle in Finnish Lappland.

The author of *Wandering, A Walker's Guide to the Mountain Trails of Europe* (1972) and the Sierra Club Book, *Huts and Hikes in the Dolomites* (1974), she has published articles in *Harper's Bazaar, Mademoiselle, The New York Times, MS., Backpacker, Ski, Skiing, Wilderness Camping,* and others. Miss Rudner attended Antioch College, and when she is not in the mountains, she lives and writes in New York City.